OCCUPANCY 250

A COLLECTION OF EINSTEIN A GO-GO
MEMORABILIA, PHOTOS AND STORIES FROM
FANS, BANDS AND FRIED CHICKEN LOVERS

Jennifer Curry Compton, Allison Durham,
Jon Glass and Dee Edenfield Marling

EAGG Press, LLC
3020 Hartley Rd., Suite 300
Jacksonville, FL 32257

eaggpress.com

ISBN 9798991283717

DEDICATED TO

The Faircloth family

Anyone who cherishes the time they spent at Einstein A Go-Go

The bands that played there

The friends who danced there

All the folks who didn't experience Einstein's firsthand, but have
been listening to our stories for nearly four decades

INTRODUCING.....
EINSTEIN
A GO-GO
327 1ST STREET NORTH
JACKSONVILLE BEACH, FL 32250
CALL 246-4073 FOR INFO

PROGRESSIVE DANCE MUSIC   A MUSIC SHOP PRODUCTION

HERE WE GO AGAIN, ANOTHER YEAR.

EINSTEIN A GO GO opened July 1985. We have welcomed new friends
and said alot of goodbyes. The club was founded for the purpose
of exposing people to music they would normally not hear. With
that in mind we have brought to Jacksonville some of the best
in recorded and live music. Bands that for a long time passed
by our neck of shopping malls.

Thanks to all of you who have faithfully supported us for
without you we could not operate. We hope you continue to do
so for a long time. We love you.

A page from the first yearbook that Tammie Faircloth put together in 1986

DEC 2 ... SONIC YOUTH &BALL

FRIDAY, DEC 3 dreams so real

SATURDAY, DEC 10 ROYAL CRESCENT MOB

IN CONCERT:

Thursday, SEPT 21 the SWANS

Friday SEPT 22 ALEX CHILTON
WITH SPECIAL GUEST: Texas Instruments

Saturday OCT 21 SCREAMING TREES
ON SST RECORDS

Saturday OCT 28 BULLET LAVOLTA
ON TAANG RECORDS

at EINSTEIN A GO-GO

SATURDAY · MAY 10 · BILLY JAMES

FRIDAY · MAY 15 · DROPPED SO SLOW

FRIDAY · MAY 22 · 3 BLIND MICE

FRIDAY · MAY 29 · NOT SHAKESPEARE

FRIDAY · JUNE 5 · FETCHIN BONES

... AND MORE, SO MUCH MORE ...

TABLE OF CONTENTS

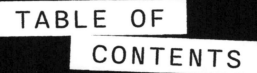

EINSTEIN A GO-GO

Friday FEB 1 JONATHAN RICHMAN

Sunday FEB 3 MARY'S DANISH

Saturday FEB 9 ALICE DONUT

Friday FEB 15 YO LA TENGO

EINSTEIN A GO-GO (PH) 249-4646

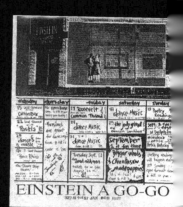

SATURDAY APRIL 11   EINSTEIN A GO GO
TWIN/TONE RECORDING ARTIST   327 N 1st ST

THE NEATS
FROM BOSTON $5

FRIDAY APRIL 17 $4
Pili-Pili
LOCAL JAZZ/REGGAE

FRIDAY APRIL 24
rubber thongs $4

WED. APRIL 22
REPLACEMENTS
with special guest : ALEX CHILTON $10

THURSDAY NOVEMBER 6 ... RAINMAKERS

SATURDAY NOVEMBER 8 ... GREAT INVISIBLES

FRIDAY NOVEMBER 14 THE FLAMING TELEPATH TOUR
SONIC YOUTH AND FIREHOSE

SATURDAY NOVEMBER 15
THREE O'CLOCK

EINSTEIN A GO-GO
327 1ST ST JAX BCH (PH) 246-4073

May
Saturday, 5 ... NIRVANA

SUNDAY, 6 ... ROBYN HITCHCOCK

Friday, 11 ... the fluid

Friday, 25 ... BEGGAR WEEDS

EINSTEIN A GO-GO
327 NORTH 1st STREET · JACKSONVILLE BEACH, FLORIDA

EINSTEIN A GOGO
327 N 1ST ST JAX BCH

SAT. 24 FLAMING LIPS

FRIDAY 30 Young Fresh Fellows

SAT. OCT. 1st alice dOnut

FRI. 7 LOVE TRACTOR

SAT. 8 DUMPTRUCK

THURS. 13 BBQ KILLERS

FRIDAY 14 NAOMIS HAIR

SAT. 15 THE LYRES

SAT. 29 LIVING COLOR

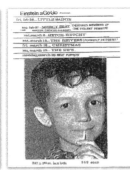

FOREWORD

Einstein A Go-Go was an all-ages club at 327 1st Street North in Jacksonville Beach, Florida. With a grand opening on July 4th, 1985, the club had a nearly 12-year run of live music, dance nights and so much more before closing in early 1997. Einstein's was the brainchild of the Faircloth family (Bill, Connie, Terri and Tammie) and had a little record shop in the back aptly named Theory Shop. The club's official capacity was 250 people, but its impact on the thousands who passed through its doors was infinite.

S EVERAL YEARS AGO, I WAS APPROACHED REGARDING A BOOK IDEA about Einstein A Go-Go and I've been writing and rewriting the foreword ever since. It's hard to put into words, let alone find the perfect words to show what a profound effect it had on me, my family and so many others. I thought I would focus on one: Gratitude.

Faces may have changed throughout the years, but the sentiment of love and support never seemed to waver. Even 27 years after the club closed, I am still totally humbled and overwhelmed each time someone stops me to say "Thank you" and to share their experiences of how much the club meant to them.

I've always said it was the combination of a perfect place and time. Everyone who crossed that threshold made an impact. There were amazing people I met along the way, awesome music emerging during that time, and the experiences of so many iconic bands live, up close and personal. More importantly, there were friendships and connections made that have lasted a lifetime.

To our extended Einstein's family, we truly couldn't have done it without you. To those close friends who helped shape us along the way, I wish I had told you more often how much that meant. Thank you, mom, dad and Terri for making it all possible.

Thank you to the tireless efforts of the authors and selfless contributors that made this project a reality. It was a true labor of love to bring these stories and pictures back to life decades later. There are not enough words to express my deep gratitude to everyone that helped to make this dream happen. I wish I could thank you all individually but that would take a lifetime (and another book!).

In closing, I haven't seen the following pages yet as I have been waiting along with the rest of you. I hope that as you flip through this book it transports you back to a time of great memories, fun stories, good friends and amazing music. Thank you for being an imprint on the love story that my family and I were so fortunate to share and for keeping EAGG alive in your hearts. I am eternally indebted to you.

Please think of our friends and loved ones that we have lost along the way. My mother and father are among them. They will be forever in our hearts.

With Love and Gratitude,
Tammie Faircloth

"I mean, it was weird to go from Einstein's in 1988 to the stadium opening for The Rolling Stones. We even dedicated a song to Einstein's because we wanted everybody to know that Einstein's was the place that gave us a chance and that the sisters were really good to us. If it wasn't for them, we wouldn't be here."

— *Corey Glover, LIVING COLOUR*

"The audience is always so important. Brian Eno has a term called 'scenious,' which is that all great art is not really made by the artist, but rather it's made by all the participants within a scene. The participants in Jacksonville were all really unique. It was a time and place in Jacksonville that happened because of a convergence of different people realizing that something needed to happen."

— Mark Cline, LOVE TRACTOR

"By opening this little punk club and their record stores, the Faircloths gave us so much. We were drifters, and they brought us into their world of music and art. They gave us something to be exhilarated about, something to look forward to, something to burrow into, and maybe most importantly, a sanctum to be outsiders."

— Shannon Wright, CROWSDELL

Einstein A Go-Go

TICKET

PIP TICKETS

No. 162

Tammie, Connie, Bill and Terri : The Faircloth family inside their live music/dance club Einstein A Go-Go, 1989

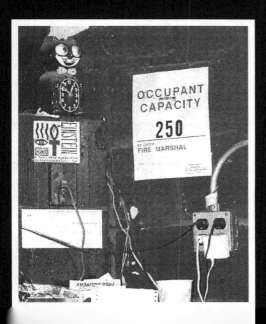

"You have to remember there was no quality college radio in the entire state back then — no internet, no place to hear anything alternative. You might hear that kind of music in a record store but not anywhere else. That's why Einstein A Go-Go was a godsend. It was the only cultural intersection that I had access to, and I treasured it."
— *Michael Brennan*

Einstein A Go-Go's original capacity was 200 and expanded to 250 when the Theory Shop

Open (weekdays) 8-2 (?) Closed New Sundays ('til summer)
(Fri-Sat) 8-12

We Do Not SERVE ALCOHOL!

Shoes, shirts AND PROPER required.

The club did not serve alcohol
so people of all ages could come

"On my first night bartending, this Navy guy was there. He had one of those short haircuts that he tried to spike up in the middle and wore the wraparound early '80s, new wave sunglasses. He asked for a Jack and Coke and I thought he said chocolate Coke (remember, Einstein's had chocolate Cokes). So I served it to him, he took a huge gulp and did a spit take over the bar."

— JOHN JONES

Drink = mc²

Poi Dog Watering (ice water)	25¢
Teeea·Lite (herbal teas)	50¢
They Might Be Java (coffee)	50¢
EiNSTEiN·a·Cocoa (hot chocolate)	75¢
Koala (orange·mango; orange·passionfruit; kiwi·lime·grapefruit; apple·blackcurrant; lemon, lime, and orange)	$1.25
N.Y. Seltzer (lemon·lime, peach, black cherry, raspberry, rootbeer, vanilla creme)	$1.25
Quibell (mineral water: raspberry·strawberry, lemon·lime, citrus, passionfruit·grapefruit)	$1.25
Moussy (Milli·Beer·illi ~ it's fake 2)	$1.25
Beatle Juice [(paul is dead now) apple, cranberry]	$1.25
Soda Pop Will Drink itself (coke, diet coke, sprite, rootbeer)	sm~75¢ lg~1.00
Chocolate or Cherry Coke	sm 1.00 lg 1.25
jules' java	75¢
HippyChuck	$1.25

May u live 2 see the dawn
menu thanx 2:
   Chuck & jules & joey

Einstein a Go Go
A MUSIC SHOP PRODUCTION·SIZZLE?

EARLY DAYS

Einstein's dance floor circa 1989

THE ORIGINS OF EINSTEIN A GO-GO

A FEW YEARS BEFORE THE CLUB OPENED I was working at our music shop in St. Augustine, ordering records, vinyl and cassettes. One day, a British guy came in and requested an album by synthpop act Landscape. When he came in to pick it up he's like, "Oh my God, you really have to hear this." We played it there in the store, and I thought that's really catchy. I only heard it that one time.

Then I started going to a club called The Blighted Area and saw 10,000 Maniacs, Minutemen, and all these great bands there. It was a really tiny dive in Jacksonville Beach. I climbed The Blighted's stairs many times and remember how soft the floors were on the second floor. It was there that I talked with bands and saw the potential of what live music could be. I thought there could be so much more than what was going on. That's where the club idea started.

My Dad had looked at a few places but it just kind of dropped. Then one day, my Dad told me he found just the right spot. We looked at it and I was like, "Oh, my gosh, this is perfect." At that time it was a teen club and breakdancing place. There were mirror tiles everywhere and mirrors all along the wall.

We decided we were going to do it, and one night my mom, dad, Terri and I were throwing around ideas for club names. I remember thinking it was a bunch of really bad names. Exhausted, I said, "I'm going up to bed." I went to sleep and then all of a sudden I woke up and said, "Einstein A Go-Go," the title of a song from that Landscape album. I ran downstairs and they were still up. "Einstein A Go-Go. That's the name, Einstein A Go-Go." It took a minute and my mom says, "You know, it's catchy." And that's how it started.

I like to say it woke me from a dream.

— *Tammie Faircloth*

Terri and Tammie Faircloth
in front of their club

Connie

"Connie was very sweet. I would ask her for advice at The Music Shop. She knew about new wave bands, punk bands, all this stuff. She would tell you, 'Oh, check this band out, check that out.' Especially now as I get older, I wonder how old she was relative to how old I am now. She was more of a grandmotherly figure in terms of the way I saw her. So you've got this kind of grandma giving you advice, like 'Hey, you should check out Gene Loves Jezebel.'"

— *Jess Bowers*

"My curfew was 10 p.m. and Connie offered to call my parents to let them know that I was in a safe place with adult supervision so they would let me stay later. It didn't work, but I never forgot how incredibly nice that was. What club owner does that?"

— *Stacy McGilvra*

"I worked at the Theory Shop until Connie died before I had my own record store in downtown Jacksonville, Moon Colony Razorblade. We literally bought out all of the remaining stock from the Theory Shop before we opened. I remember she would talk about the newest records and which ones she liked. She kept up with music and everything that was going on until her dying day. "

— CASH CARTER

"My mother Connie was an only child and my dad was orphaned at an early age. I think the family atmosphere stemmed from them wanting to have a place where they felt like they and others could belong."

— Terri Faircloth

Bill

"I can still see Mr. Faircloth backstage over a frying pan and pots of black beans and rice. One night, I shared his cave kitchen, frantically tuning guitars. He came from around the stove and said, 'You've got to tune down and then bring it back up to the right note.' He grasped the headstock and demonstrated a smooth correction and I never forgot."

— ADAM WATSON,
Beggar Weeds

"I remember Bill's drink machine, our abuse of it, and him letting us know we'd crossed the line with his generosity."

— BEN REYNOLDS
Chickasaw Mudd Puppies

BACKSTAGE WITH BILL

EINSTEIN'S HAD TWO BACKSTAGE areas, a large room downstairs shared by staff, and a smaller room upstairs where the bands could have some privacy. Upstairs was called the Crow's Nest, a small space of unfinished brick walls, a few chairs and two windows that looked out over the Atlantic Ocean. Downstairs was just off the stage behind a curtain and stuffed with rock venue and record store ephemera: old lights and mic stands, fliers, mannequins, boxes of T-shirts, racks of LPs, decommissioned turntables and assorted sound equipment. Everything was dusty and a bit musty, with a distinct sour smell of ocean water intrusion, frying oil, sweat, patchouli and pipe tobacco. It was the sort of smell you never forget.

Bill Faircloth and I cooked and served dinner for the bands and their crews from 1986-1989. In the back of the downstairs area Bill had fashioned himself a little kitchen of sorts. He had a mini fridge for meats and veg and his beloved Budweisers, a makeshift prep table, a small sink and a couple electric hot plates. He was an accomplished cook and made dinner for all the traveling bands. He said he wanted to make sure they got a home-cooked meal while on the road.

He was in his early 60s then, tall and very thin, missing most of his hair and teeth, but always smartly dressed in a tweed flat cap and cardigan. Bands I've run into since then always remember him and his food. I cooked a little too, but mostly ran errands for groceries or to pick up beer at The Ritz, a small biker bar known then for dwarf tossing and sidewalk brawls. I'd cut through an empty, weeded lot, stepping over broken glass and used condoms and syringes. The Ritz had a package store back then, and a six-pack of Budweiser cost about four dollars. I'd get some for Bill and some for the bands. I don't remember ever offering liquor to the bands — maybe because EAGG was all-ages with no license to sell — but Tammie and I sometimes dipped into Dad's beer when he wasn't looking. Perched on his homemade stool with a pipe in hand, Bill's eyes would crinkle with suspicion at our antics but he rarely intervened.

> **Tammie and I sometimes dipped into Dad's beer when he wasn't looking.**

I coordinated the menu with the band's rider and figured out the timing of service. Food was usually served after soundcheck. The band and crew ate first, then staff. Bill usually made enough for everyone: spaghetti or fried fish, mashed potatoes and gravy, black beans and rice, green beans or a salad. When the stove went in later he'd do a pot roast with carrots and biscuits or a big pot of soup. The meals were served on paper plates or bowls, with plastic forks and paper towels. The bands lined up at the service table and we filled the plates and passed them over. The surprise on their faces made all the effort worth it, their gratitude palpable. Feeding people is loving them, especially when the food was this good. The bands were effusive in their thanks, their compliments. It connected us to them, and them to each other, a communal breaking of the bread. A good meal does that. Bill did that.

Bill's ace — his workhorse — was a vintage electric frying pan. What's your best memory of biting into the perfect piece of fried chicken? Now imagine you're in a touring band, stuffed into the back of a smelly van for weeks, subsisting on gas station snacks and fast food. Touring in the States is a brain-numbing slog that barely earns you enough to get to the next town. A decent hotel room is expensive, showers are rare, and a good home-cooked meal will bring a big man to his knees. Anthony Kiedis and Flea from the Red Hot Chili Peppers were so overcome they both immediately burst into song and started humping my leg. Mike Patton of Faith No More and Chris Robinson later of The Black Crowes visibly choked up. Soul Asylum, Jane's Addiction and 10,000 Maniacs came back for seconds. They always did. I wish I still had the recipe for that chicken, but Bill created something back there in his makeshift kitchen that I'll never forget. It felt like family.

— Shawn Barton Vach

Shawn Barton Vach worked at Einstein's from 1986-1989

"THE FAIRCLOTH SISTERS ARE TO OUR COMMUNITY what Kerrygold Butter is to food. You don't see the butter in the food because it melts and becomes part of everything. But it enhances the flavors of everything and brings the flavors together. So, you get your garlic and basil, melt them in the Kerrygold Butter, and you get your synchronicity. They had very little ego and no greed about them. They did it selflessly. If they were jerks, they could have made a whole lot more money. But it was never really about the money."

—Shelton Hull

"From 1984 to '85, I had been at school at FSU, but I'd come home and was helping in The Music Shop. Tammie was talking about opening a club and I thought, 'OK, let's see what we can do with it. Count me in and I'll do whatever you need me to do.' Our dad was really instrumental in bringing the club to life. He was a very talented carpenter and put his spin on building the stage, the bar area and the booths. It was a lot of grunt work in the beginning, but Tammie had a great group of friends that helped. We had connections for getting sound equipment and setting all that up, and the bands gave us guidance on how to set up the monitors. It was definitely a learning process."

— *Terri Faircloth*

Terri

"I remember talking to Terri a lot. She was like that bartender you could talk to about your problems and she would give you some good advice."

– *Michael Virzera*

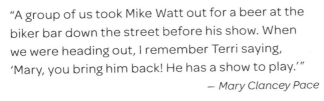

"A group of us took Mike Watt out for a beer at the biker bar down the street before his show. When we were heading out, I remember Terri saying, 'Mary, you bring him back! He has a show to play.'"

— *Mary Clancey Pace*

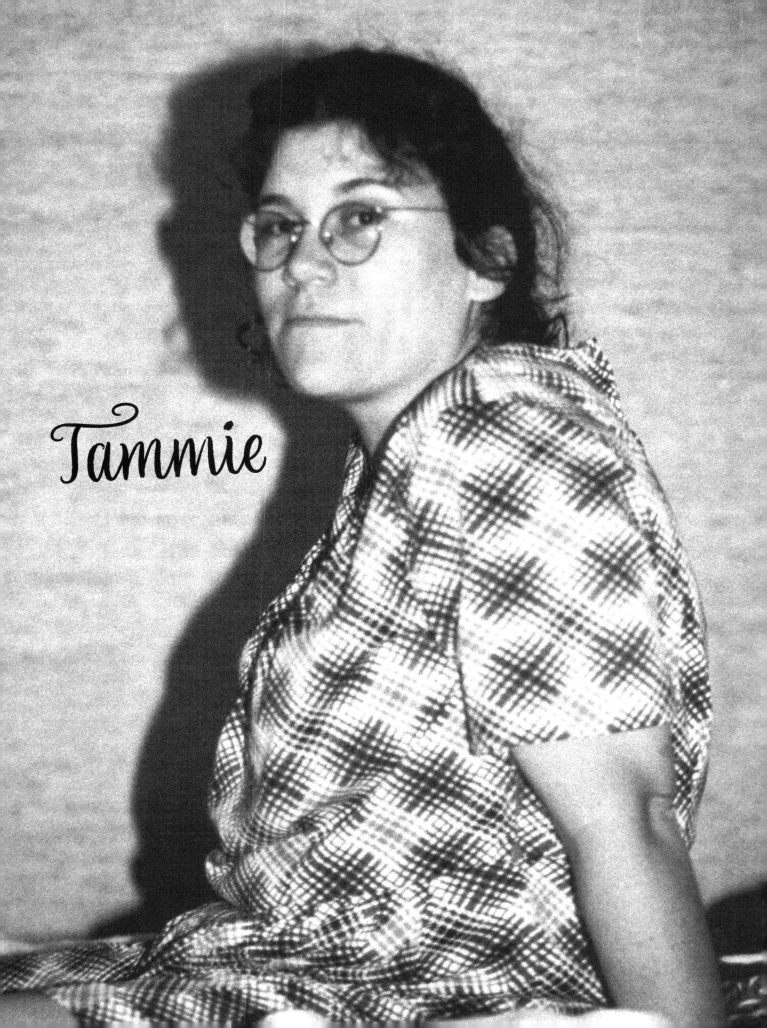

Tammie

"I was just a kid who was always in the shop hanging out buying records. Hell, I would come in to hang out with Tammie before work because she was so much fun. We'd shoot the shit and talk music."

— BRYAN MASSEY

"One time I went to the store with Tammie to pick up 'fog juice.' I was blown away that they had so many 'flavors' (or really that there were flavors?). If I recall correctly, the flavor they used was a bespoke one called Gothic Paradise. Tammie said, 'It was actually vanilla.' I replied, 'Yes, but doesn't Gothic Paradise make a better story?'"

— Jess Bowers

Tammie at the Athens Music Festival, 1988

"When I turned 18, my mom kicked me out the day after I graduated. I'd already been a regular at the club, so I started going from open to close. Some kids and I got a house in Riverside, but I knew my safe place was at EAGG. I was like a stray dog that hated everyone but when Tammie took me in and hired me at the club, I felt welcomed. My hate went away. There was always more to it than just a place to hang or the music, or at least in my heart it was. There was a family aspect about it. And there still is. Thanks, Tammie and the Faircloth family. Love you all!"

— Sonny Thigpen

Designing fliers in her apartment

YOU'D BETTER CHECK YOURSELF

ONE OF THE THINGS I REALLY appreciated, especially now that I'm older and have a kid, is whenever somebody around the club got too big of an ego, Tammie would make sure she grounded them by sticking a note to the back of their shirt without them noticing or putting toilet paper on the back of their pants. Sometimes she'd carry around this poster tube with a little needle on the end of it and poke them whenever they were talking to a girl or whatever. She'd do all these different little things to pull them back down to reality. That was something about Tammie I was afraid of back then. Anytime she came around with a camera I knew she was going to try to embarrass me. I ran from her camera, but I think there are still a few pictures of me in the last couple of yearbooks.

I worked with Tammie for years and one time I asked her if she was doing those things to keep us grounded. She was like, "Oh, yeah, of course. I'd see some of you guys out there getting too big of a head or treating some of the women like crap and so I put you in your place."

— *Cash Carter*

POLES BABY

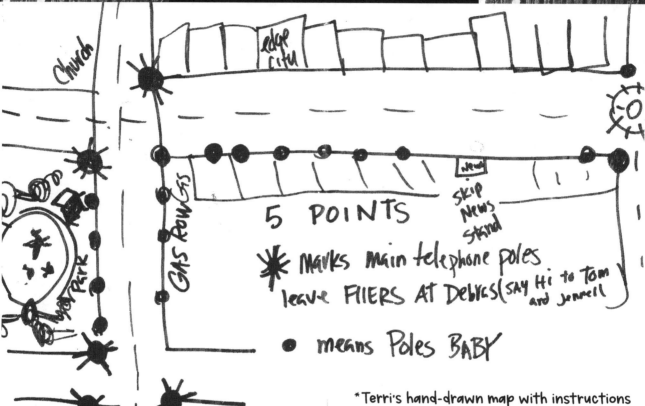

*Terri's hand-drawn map with instructions

"Tammie and Terri would do marketing on Mondays and Tuesdays when the club was closed. Usually under the cover of night, we ran around the empty sidewalks of the trendy Five Points neighborhood, hanging fliers and posters on telephone poles. Occasionally we had to explain ourselves to the police, and once in a while would run into Tom and Gunnel from Edge City. After our adventure, we would feed the ducks at the pond in Riverside Park."

— Allison Durham

Einstein
A GOGO

NEW MUSIC CLUB

Grand Opening
JULY 4th

BETWEEN MUSIC SHOP AND
OLD BLIGHTED. 3RD ST, JAX BEACH

NO ALCOHOL INSIDE

OPEN-LATE! 7-4AM

WITH MUSICAL GUESTS

HORSECHILD BREAKFAST

THE FIRST NIGHT, THE FIRST TASTE

WHILE MY OLDER FRIENDS AND siblings had a club called The Blighted Area where they could go to sing songs of drink and dance and music, the younger ones were stuck at home with turntables, cassettes and maybe a fanzine. We were left to imagine a life sharing the new inspiring decadent, alternative sounds that drew us away from the metal and glam music that permeated the radio at that time.

In mid-1985, as we suffered through the beginning of high school, skate punk and new wave music were just hitting our psyches. It seemed yet another lot borne of angst-ridden youth would be defined by belligerence, vandalism and truancy. Then July 4, 1985, rolled around.

On that day, an alternative came to life that would become an escape, a haven, a sanctuary. I heard from my older brothers that something was going to happen on First and Third streets at the beach, Jax Beach, that would offer a youthful all-aged adventure.

And so, mid-afternoon that day I went there, youngest brother in tow, to wait several hours for the club to open. No one knew at the time that this place would see thousands of kids enter a world that was designed for them. A world they never knew existed, but they craved for survival. It was like a Kafka parable, but with a happy ending.

> ## That night was the beginning of a moment in life we would forever look back on.

I felt settled and comfortable in this world that would become my second home —a place that would give me a job, family and friends I would keep forever.

When Einstein A Go-Go opened that night the people coming in couldn't possibly fathom that a legend was being born. An infancy of confusion bearing acceptance of quandary. A dance of mindful happiness and cacophonous energy.

That night was the beginning of a moment in life we would forever look back on. Like parents who shaped us, teachers who taught us, friends who guided us, that night was the ultimate lesson in life, where reality began and life started to come to fruition.

Were it not for the music, the people, the visionaries (you know who you are) and the simple camaraderie that were brought together that night, we all would have ended up elsewhere — some dead, others oppressed, many still closeted — likely never having filled a void. That first taste of Einstein's, I think we can all agree, was the opening to a world most people in the same type of small town would be very jealous of.

Out of those of us alive today, many likely still are because of a club that opened the night of July 4 in 1985.

— *Jeffrey Totty*

Jeffrey Totty was at Einstein's on opening night

COME ON GET HAPPY

"The Tottys were customers at our music store at Regency across from the mall. That's where I met Celeste, Jan, Jay, Jeffrey and Joel. They were like the Partridge Family because they were all so different, but they were very hip."

— *Tammie Faircloth*

HEYDAYS WITH
HORSECHILD
BREAKFAST

I N HIS BOOK *OUTLIERS*, MALCOLM Gladwell underlines the importance of timing and "where we came from" in mapping our paths. Some of us spent our youths romanticizing our parents' generation only to realize much later that we grabbed the brass ring in the '80s in Jacksonville Beach.

We rehearsed in the club for a while prior to the opening and then still rehearsed there on weekdays before moving to the practice place next door. So much was condensed into such a relatively short time period.

The Faircloth family and their haven of a beach dive initiated us and multiplied all possibilities. For those drawn to drive to Jacksonville Beach as often as time and wallets would afford, Einstein A Go-Go rewarded us with a place of nurture and challenge, much more than our homes or a football game or a booth at Bennigan's.

It was a fantastic 15 minutes for all of us. We met our heroes and made lasting friendships.

— *Horsechild Breakfast*

Scott Leuthold and Adam Watson rock Einstein A Go-Go's first anniversary party, July 4, 1986

Palmer Wood

Alan Cowart

LOVE
TRACTOR

"WHEN EINSTEIN'S OPENED IT WAS THIS BEACON,
A LIGHTHOUSE OF SOMETHING HAPPENING IN FLORIDA."

THE MUSIC SHOP PRESENTS:

LOVE TRACTOR

FRIDAY JULY 12TH

PLUS SPECIAL GUEST: HORSE CHILD BREAKFAST

EINSTEIN a go go
327 1ST ST N

A NEW THEORY IN ENTERTAINMENT

MUSIC SHOP   1ST ST EAST   BLIGHTED AREA

NO ALCOHOL PERMITTED

Ph 216 4073 FOR INFO

"WE WERE BOOKED AT EINSTEIN'S

AND THE NAME SOUNDED WEIRD. But when we got there, we realized this was our kind of place. I remember being impressed by how knowledgeable the audience was when it came to music and how dedicated they were. They were outsiders and this was their clubhouse."
— Mark Cline, LOVE TRACTOR

Mike Richmond

Armistead Wellford

Mark Cline

Andrew Carter

BASSIST ARMISTEAD WELLFORD recalls how Love Tractor's future producer Pat Irwin joined their road trip from Athens to Jacksonville Beach to determine if the band was ready to sign with Big Time/RCA Records: *"At Einstein's we could express ourselves and not feel intimidated or like we were faking it because we'd been playing there for years. Afterward, Pat was like, 'I think we should do this.' That was an important part of our history and I'll never forget that."*

THE jayLIST

Jay Totty talks about
Einstein A Go-Go and
DJing the first year

EINSTEIN'S OPEN
ARMS PHILOSOPHY

*"The club had a
lot of different
ages and diversity.
Anyone was
welcome and
that's a vital
message to
send out."*

"WORLD DESTRUCTION" John Lydon & Afrika Bambaataa • "PERFECT SKIN" Lloyd Cole & the Commotions • "CITIES IN DUST" Siouxsie & the Banshees • "SHE SELLS SANCTUARY" The Cult • "LET'S GO TO BED" The Cure • "HOW SOON IS NOW?" The Smiths • "THE CUTTER" Echo and the Bunnymen • "THIS CHARMING MAN" The Smiths • "LOVE CATS" The Cure • "TAINTED LOVE" Soft Cell • "TRANSMISSION" Joy Division • "TEMPTATION" New Order • "I WILL DARE" The Replacements • "BLACK LILIES" Fetchin' Bones • "HEAVEN" The Psychedelic Furs • "RADIO FREE EUROPE" R.E.M. • "TRAIN IN VAIN (STAND BY ME)" The Clash • "BELA LUGOSI'S DEAD" Bauhaus • "SENSES WORKING OVERTIME" XTC • "LOVE WILL TEAR US APART" Joy Division • "DON'T LEAVE ME THIS WAY" The Communards • "UNCERTAIN SMILE" The The • "NEMESIS" Shriekback

"This playlist is a combination of crowd-pleasers that packed the dance floor, as well as some other songs I played."

— JAY TOTTY

CLEANING CREW

"I was a DJ but I was also the janitor. I started fetching ice and cleaning the bathroom. If you could stick around for those two things and talk about music, you were welcomed."

LIFE ON THE DANCE FLOOR

"It was so much fun and so much joy to be able to just dance your heart out."

THE SIGNIFICANCE OF BEING ALL AGES

"Being all ages, all the time, was really important because so many young people would never have had a chance to see all those bands. It opened up a huge window for kids, and it was a real leap to have that kind of vision and make it work for so long."

WEARING SKIRTS

"I'm sure there was a part of me that said, 'You know, this will be a little different, but whatever.' But after a short period of time, it was something that I didn't even think about. Skirts are comfortable, I'll tell you that."

BikTHAY BASH JULY 4TH

WHEN WE ROLLED UP TO LOAD IN ON the Fourth, a trio of gangly kids were carrying equipment through the parking lot. One was taking a pair of drumsticks to every car and beating out rhythms on the club façade with energy to burn. He was a caffeinated waif, or to paraphrase Gibby Haynes and Butthole Surfers, a "sausage that dances like Ray Bolger on the hood of a car in a traffic jam."

This was a 13-year-old Ian Chase, the bass player for R.O.K. the opening band for the evening. He and the Gentry brothers (Brannon and Mark) would later change their name to Rein Sanction, sign to Sub Pop, and alter our aural landscape far beyond the Dinosaur Jr. crate into which major labels wanted to cram them.

— *Scott Leuthold, HORSECHILD BREAKFAST*

THE BANDS

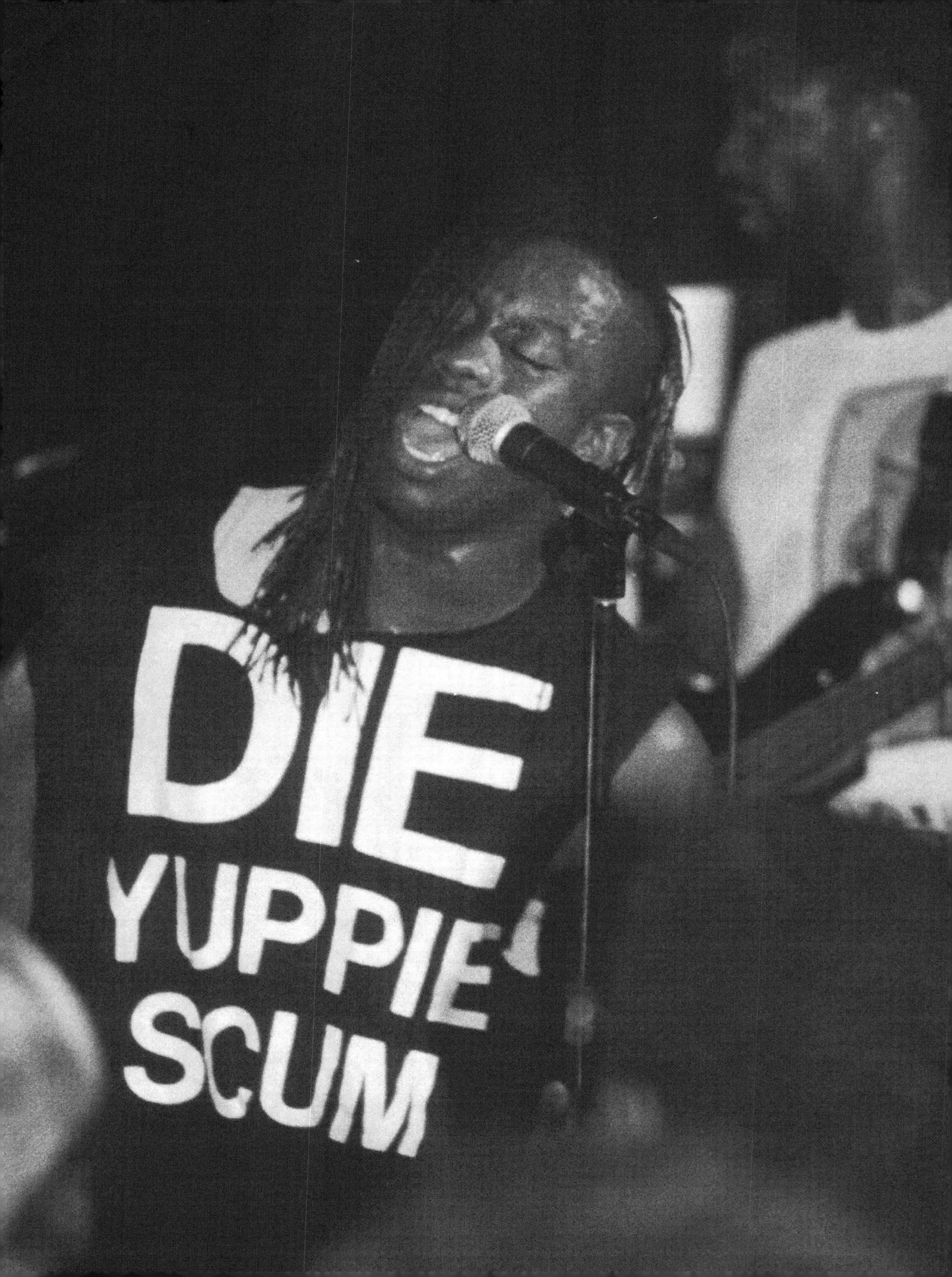
DIE
YUPPIE
SCUM

TAKING CENTER STAGE

THE BAND LIST SPEAKS VOLUMES. You know, the list. The one that graces many of your Einstein's T-shirts. The one that grew a little bigger and a little bolder with each yearbook. The list that appears on the back cover of this very book.

How exactly that storied list came to be over a dozen years was truly about keeping promises. In the early days, Jacksonville Beach was not exactly on the circuit for touring acts. Tammie credits a referral from the guys in the band Love Tractor to the now legendary booking agent Frank Riley. The Faircloths guaranteed Frank one thing: If bands made the out-of-the way trek to north Florida, they would leave with money in hand.

"Even if we didn't make the money at the door, you still had to pay that person," Tammie says. "You can't just say, 'Oh well, here's some beer.' Bands knew that if you played Einstein's you were going to get paid."

With that promise, Frank started steering acts such as The dB's, Violent Femmes and Meat Puppets to the beachfront musical outpost and others started to follow suit. Modern English booked the club for a week in 1986 as a practice spot for their upcoming tour and played open mic night under an alias. The Replacements launched their 1987 tour at Einstein's a couple months before the release of *Pleased to Meet Me*. 10,000 Maniacs made three appearances before MTV fame whisked them away to larger theaters and arenas.

Acts found themselves loving Einstein's for more than just the guarantee. To Camper Van Beethoven bassist Victor Krummenacher, the Faircloths served up tried-and-true Southern hospitality that always made him and his bandmates feel welcomed.

"At that point, we were playing The Rathskeller in Boston and CBGB in New York," says Victor. "Then you'd go someplace where people were nice to you and brought you home-cooked food. We would remember that and try to be loyal to those places for as long as we could."

As alternative music found its way into the mainstream, the names got bigger — or at least seemingly so, in retrospect — Red Hot Chili Peppers. Jane's Addiction. Nirvana. While opening for The The in 1993, The Cranberries jumped off that tour to play a sweat-soaked summer night at the club. In the span of a year, Living Colour went from Einstein's to opening for The Rolling Stones at the Gator Bowl.

"We even dedicated a song to Einstein's because we wanted everybody to know that Einstein's was the place that gave us a chance and that the sisters were really good to us," says Living Colour's Corey Glover. "If it wasn't for them, we wouldn't be here."

— *Jon Glass*

Corey Glover,
Living Colour, 1988

10,000 MANIACS

"I am so fortunate that my daddy was the coolest ever! He let me go to two of the 10,000 Maniacs shows at Einstein's. I was 10 or 11 at the time and adored Natalie Merchant. As a little girl with similar features and growing up in a small town with very little diversity, she was inspiring and helped me through times of alienation.

I got to chat with Natalie on both occasions — against all odds, and strange to me as I usually felt invisible. She remembered meeting me, which let me know that even if I felt out of place and easily forgotten, that's not how other people saw me. She touched my face and later, when it all struck me, I cried.

If you've ever felt like the young me — and at times, the adult me — please remember: You are awesome! You are loved! You've made an impression on people in ways you may never know. So, be kind to yourself."

— *Sondra Stellaria*

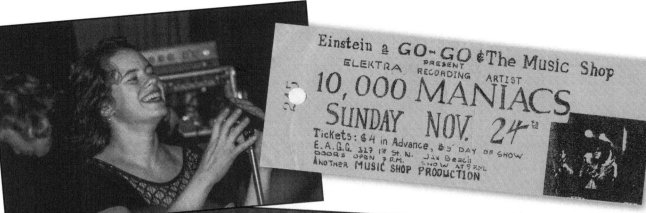

"When I was 16 and asked my mom for tickets to 10,000 Maniacs, she said 'I will not let my daughter see a band with a name like that.' A year later she bought me tickets to Nirvana."

— *Mary Donovan*

"10,000 Maniacs was my first show at Einstein's — the second time when they played for *In My Tribe*. I worked at a flower shop and there were mixed cut flowers left over from arrangements that were going to be thrown out so I asked if I could have them. I gave Natalie about 200 flowers in a bucket. During the show she said 'Robby and Ralph gave me all these flowers but I don't deserve them, so I want to share them with you all.' The whole dance floor and stage were covered in flowers. It was so cool to see flowers everywhere."

— ROBERT ARMSTRONG

Natalie Merchant and Steve Gustafson, 1987

"I must admit I've had a crush on Natalie Merchant since I first heard her sing."

— JOHN JONES

"In 1985, 10,000 Maniacs came to my parents' house in Mandarin before one of their early shows at The Blighted Area. My grandmother answered the door and told me there were some Jehovah's Witnesses there to see me (no one knew them at that point). Natalie told me they might make $7 a day, mostly from the self-produced records they were selling out of the van — actually, not bad money compared with what we made daily. Todd and I hung out with her quite a bit. Years later when they were a much bigger indie band and played probably one of their last club shows at Einstein's, I went up to say hi, wondering if she would even acknowledge me. But she immediately hugged and kissed me then took me backstage with the rest of the band. It's crazy now to be shopping at Target or somewhere and suddenly hear her singing. I never knew she would become such a huge international star."

— ADAM WATSON, *Beggar Weeds*

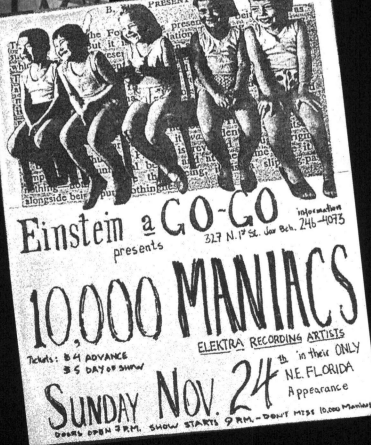

EINSTEIN A GO GO PRESENTS:

10,000 MANIACS
ON ELEKTRA RECORDS

with special guest: The Connells

$15

Sunday, Dec
13th

EINSTEIN A
GO GO
327 N 1st ST, Jax Bch
249 4646

"I loved how raw it was and how I thought Natalie was literally going
to spin herself into the ground. I've never seen a performer do that."

— James McCaffrey

THE FIRST WAVE   THE BANDS

Bill Schunk

Steve Almass & Dan Prater

BEAT RODEO ON IRS RECORDS

Lewis King

BEAT RODEO

Dan Prater

48

Michael Gira

Jarboe and Michael Gira

CAMPFIRE SONGS

AS A YOUNG TOURING BAND IN THE MID 1980s, it was exciting to get to play in Florida at all. We were in the process of visiting the whole USA, most of which was new to us as Californians. It was exotic. We thought the weather was nice enough and were pretty psyched that tropical storms were gonna be coming up the coast. We drove to the shore and parked. We went swimming and did a little bodysurfing, but we didn't have much time because we had to get to a radio interview at a local college station. When we came out of the interview it started to rain, and it was huge drops of warm rain. We ran to the van, but we got soaked and the parking lot was a pool. Exotic! At least it was warm.

Jonathan Segel

We made it over to Einstein A Go-Go and loaded in, set up and ate nearby — nice people, good area. The show was good! People showed up! We played some electric Camper Van Beethoven for about 30 minutes. Then the storm that had been coming in hit hard and the power went out. The sound of the electric guitars and violin and voices died immediately. Chris Pedersen continued on un-mic'ed drums for a second in total darkness.

Well, I guess we could wait a few minutes? Einstein's people rounded up a few flashlights. We had just done a few acoustic numbers at the radio station, so we had the acoustic guitar and mandolin in the gear. We waited about 15 minutes for power, then gave up on that. The audience wanted more music and we weren't ready to stop, so we gathered on the front of the stage. Chris wrapped his snare in a towel and sat with it and a tambourine and we divided up the acoustic instruments — Greg and Victor on guitars, David on mandolin. I could play the violin unplugged and we could still sing.

So we played the show in the dark acoustically with the audience and Einstein A Go-Go people holding flashlights. It was one of the best and most memorable shows of the tour.

— JONATHAN SEGEL, *Camper Van Beethoven*

CAMPER VAN BEETHOVEN

Photo by Edie

CAMPER VAN BEETHOVEN
SATURDAY, AUGUST 16
EINSTEIN A GO-GO - 327 N 1 ST ST. JAX BCH

№ 120

pip tickets

CAMPER VAN BEETHOVEN
with SPOT 1019

No. 189

pip tickets

WEDNESDAY, JUNE 8, 1988   10pm $8.00

David Lowery

Victor Krummenacher

Greg Lisher

"I thought it was one of the coolest things I'd ever seen at a show. Players so dedicated to their art and audience that they pulled out flashlights and acoustics."

— *Mikey Mayhem*

FLOWERS
O! DEATH
TANIA
EYE #1
#2
FRUIT
SWEETHARTS
JO STALIN
WASTED
SKIN BOWL
SHUT US DOWN
LOTTERY
THE LOSER
SWEET VIRGINA
[FOR] I MET YOU
ACOUSTIC
OPEAING
SLW
ONE OF THESE DAYS
TURQUOISE

WAKA
MATCH
MACO
UTAH
GOOD GUYS
LIFE
SHE DIVINES

"The night the lights went out we just kind of went for it. I remember the reception being really good. I don't know why, but people kind of expect you to give up. One thing Camper doesn't do very well is give up, especially in that kind of context. So for this, it's like, no, we're just going to do it."

— VICTOR KRUMMENACHER,
Camper Van Beethoven

Camper Van Beethoven's
acoustic set during a
power outage, 1989

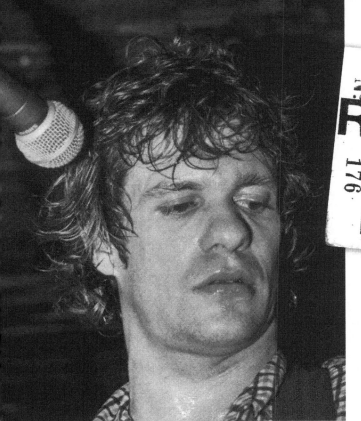

Paul Westerberg

THE MUSIC SHOP PRESENTS:

No. 176. REPLACEMENTS tickets
with special guest ALEX CHILTON
EINSTEIN A GO GO

"I remember while watching Alex Chilton play,
Paul Westerberg turned around, asked for a light,
and then gave me a fabulous wink."

— *Pat O'Brien*

Chris Mars

Tommy Stinson

"Chris Mars and Bob Weston both left the stage and
refused to come back out. Tommy Stinson and Paul
Westerberg weren't done fucking around, so Paul
asked if anyone in the crowd played the drums. Robin
Page was next to me and yelled that I was a drummer.
I remember being picked up and shoved onstage by
a couple of people. We played one 'blues exploration'
number and I got down. The stooge that got up after me
was tackled by Chris and Bob and the drums exploded."

— ALAN COWART, *Beggar Weeds*

"We learned 'Johnny's Gonna Die,' the only ballad from the first Replacements album. We thought it would be hilarious to play it opening for the band at Einstein's, but we didn't get the gig. The Replacements announced that Alex Chilton would be opening the shows on that leg of the tour."

— *Alan Cowart, Beggar Weeds*

Alex Chilton, 1987

"Alex Chilton definitely improved my outlook on a bad day."
— CHRISTOPHER HOOKER

BACK, READY FOR ACTION:

REPLACEMENTS
with special guest:
ALEX CHILTON

WED. 22
APRIL
DOORS OPEN 9PM

$10

FOR MORE
INFORMATION
CALL
246-4073
*

EINSTEIN A GO GO
327 N 1ST ST, JAX BCH
(PH) 249-4646
a music shop production
jacksonville beach · fla

"God speed Alex Chilton. I saw you first many moons ago at EAGG."
— *W. David Foster*

the reivers

John Croslin, Garrett Williams and Kim Longacre, 1989

John Croslin

Kim Longacre

Cindy Toth

THE DEAD MILKMEN

Thursday Oct. 1, 1987

Joe Jack Talcum, Rodney Anonymous and Dave Blood

Dean Clean

"Einstein A Go-Go was one of the best. I liked the clubs that didn't have age restrictions. A younger audience definitely made it better. At least 50% of any show is the audience, and I don't think we had one bad show at Einstein's."

— JOE JACK TALCUM, *The Dead Milkmen*

Joe Jack Talcum

"My brother talked to them and they needed a ride. I was maybe 13 at the time. So it was like, there's The Dead Milkmen in my mom's brown station wagon. They ended up becoming one of my favorite bands."

— EMILY WILDER, *Wet & Reckless*

The Dead Milkmen, 1987

MIRACLE LEGION

"The first thing that struck me was the family vibe because we played a lot of real dives where no one cared about you. So wow, this place is friendly and nice and not scary. And the hospitality was amazing. I remember the seafood platter after the gig with all kinds of oysters and stuff. It was a good break from the dumps we played most of the time, and then we could go dive into the surf at 2 in the morning.

I have this theory that we were all part of the one generation who never realized that you should quit — like we had this idea that we could just keep doing it. You didn't have to have a big record deal. We weren't rock stars. We weren't making money. But in our world, we were something. I think we were at a blessed time in music."

— *Ray Neal, MIRACLE LEGION*

Ray Neal

Mark Mulcahy and Ray Neal

Only a lucky few were present that night to see the "Miracle Cubes" show

MIRACLE LEGION + THE SUGARCUBES = *MIRACLE CUBES*

Myles Mangino, Ray Neal, Drew Waters, Þór Eldon (of The Sugarcubes), Mark Mulcahy and Margrét Örnólfsdóttir (also of The Sugarcubes)

Drew Waters, Ray Neal and Þór Eldon (of The Sugarcubes)

"In September 1988, we were on tour with The Sugarcubes, and we had a few days off. The Sugarcubes were taking it all in, unleashed in America and ready for whatever. So when we said we were going to play this gig in Jacksonville Beach, a few of them just dove in the van and came with us."

— *Ray Neal, MIRACLE LEGION*

"We could play six shows in Florida and Einstein's was the only place that felt like a normal gig. They really knew the music, were lovely and welcoming. I loved to play there, loved being by the ocean, loved being in weirdo Florida."

— MARK MULCAHY, *Miracle Legion*

Einstein's presents
Sonic Youth
$5.50 adv.
$6.50 door
with fIREHOSE
Naomi's Hair
Wednesday
Nov. 12
9 PM

Sonic Youth, 1988

Kim Gordon

Lee Ranaldo

Steve Shelley

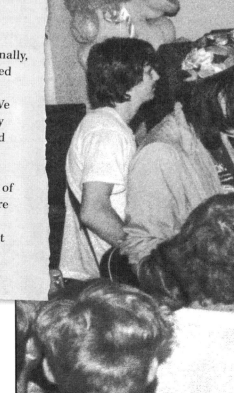

"I'd heard about Einstein's from friends in college, but hadn't gone because we wanted to hit the dance clubs that served alcohol. Finally, someone convinced me to go there to see Sonic Youth. We arrived just as they started playing and decided to hang outside and save ourselves the price of the ticket. They were so loud we were waiting for the front doors to blow off."
— HAROLD GEORGE

Thurston Moore

SONIC YOUTH
fIREHOSE

With ex-Minutemen Mike & George and Ed from Ohio

SST Records presents
The Flaming Telepath Tour

Friday, November 14
doors open at 8 pm
$6 advance
$7 day of show
Einstein-A-Go-Go
327 N. 1st St. Jax Beach
246-4073

SONIC YOUTH
fIREHOSE 14th
FRIDAY · NOVEMBER
$6 advance · $7 day of show
EINSTEIN A GO-GO 327 N 1ST ST. JAX BCH

THE FLAMING TELEPATH TOUR

Sonic Youth and fIREHOSE, 1986

"Mike Watt might be one of the coolest people alive. He signed a bass guitar for me one night after a show; however, he wouldn't sign it until he had an opportunity to play it."

— *Troy Towsley*

"My best memory from that exact spot was the night I went to see fIREHOSE and they were sold out. I was sittin' there all pissed off and Mike Watt walked out and said, 'What's the matter, son?' I told him, then he grabbed my shirt, stood me up, and commenced to walk me to their merch table. He said, 'Sell some T-shirts, and you and your friends can all see the show.' Freakin' awesome night it was. The girl I had taken was pretty damn impressed as well!"

—JO SPENCE

George Hurley, Mike Watt, Thurston Moore (in DJ booth) and Ed Crawford

fIREHOSE: George Hurley, Mike Watt and Ed Crawford

Mike Watt

George Hurley

"In 1984 we did a tour for Minutemen's *Double Nickels on the Dime* and we played The Blighted Area. This was a bizarre, insane, zombieland kind of place. The Blighted Area was the perfect name. Next time I came to Jacksonville Beach was with fIREHOSE, opening for Sonic Youth and what I really strongly remember is the fried chicken. I can smell it now."

—*Mike Watt, fIREHOSE*

Ed Crawford

The Theory Shop Presents;
IN CONCERT

MIKE WATT
and the Crew of the Flying Saucer
Wednesday, Oct 18 1995 9 PM
$7.50

Einstein A Go-Go 327 N 1st St Jax Bch

Scott Starratt,
Cameron White,
Mike Watt,
John Hafner,
Wade Starratt
and Eli Bajalia

"There was a terrible storm and above the stage, apparently there was a leak. I remember they taped plastic above the stage and it was filling with water. Here we are, musicians, with all this electronic gadgetry thinking this is how people get electrocuted. But I'm still here to tell the story.

I remember the club was instrumental in making me feel comfortable. There were sisters and one of them did sound and the music-oriented stuff while the other was doing craft services. In the dressing room there was a constant supply of goodies to eat and that's what really set them apart because at most clubs there'd be a bag of Doritos, some salsa and a six pack of beer. She was actually dipping strawberries into chocolate. When you're a band on tour, comforts are few and far between. So things like that really stand out."

— WILLIAM TUTTON, *The Geraldine Fibbers*

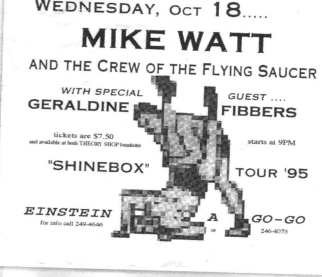

in concert

Thursday, Oct 12 .....

TUSCADERO with Hollow Nerve
starts at 9PM $4.50 at the door

WEDNESDAY, OCT 18 .....

MIKE WATT
AND THE CREW OF THE FLYING SAUCER

WITH SPECIAL
GERALDINE

GUEST ....
FIBBERS

tickets are $7.50
and available at both THEORY SHOP locations

starts at 9PM

"SHINEBOX"

TOUR '95

EINSTEIN
for info call 249-4646

A

GO-GO
or
246-4073

68

FRIDAY, JUNE 20 • 10PM •

pip tickets

SLASH RECORDING ARTIST:

BODEANS

brought TO YOU by THE MUSIC SHOP

EINSTEIN a∾ GO-GO... 327 N 1ST ST Jax BCH

Nº 106

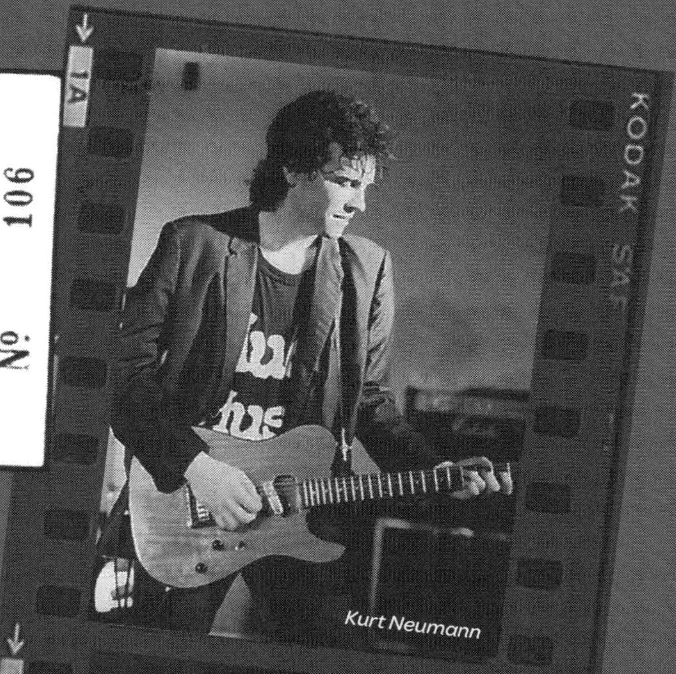

Kurt Neumann

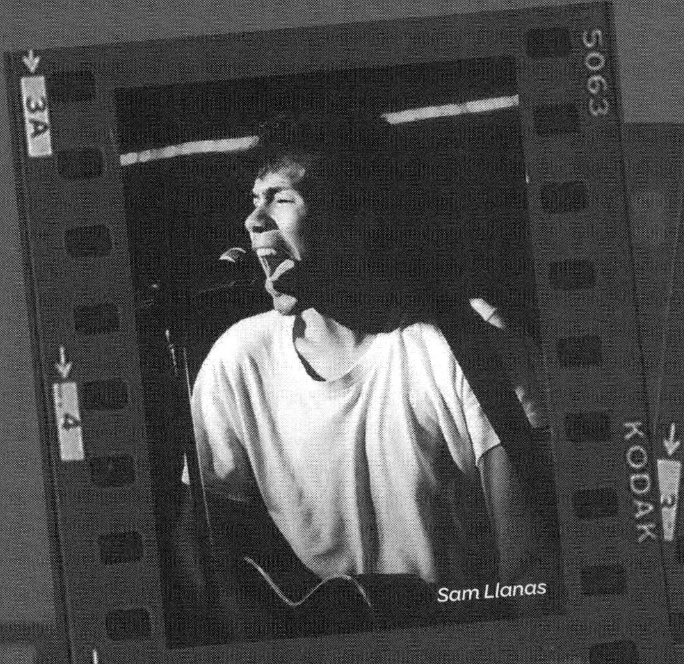

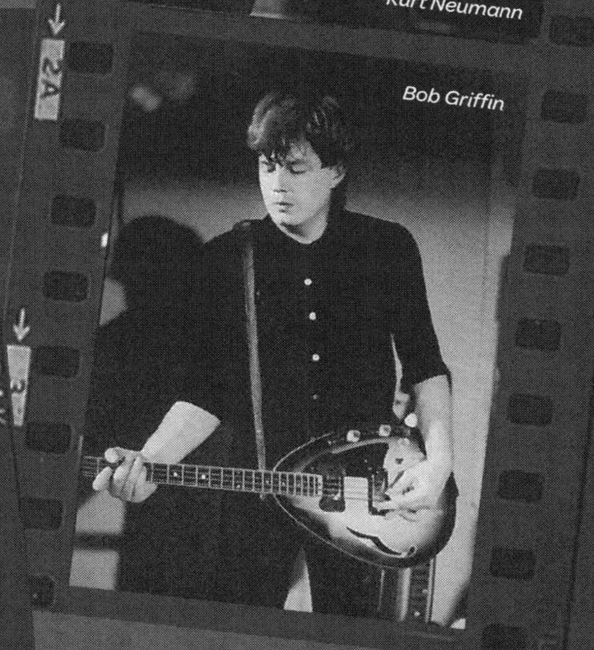

Bob Griffin

Sam Llanas

Guy Hoffman

"I remember the night I saw the BoDeans. Funny, they're still in my rotation on iTunes."

— MICHAEL LONG

BEGGAR WEEDS

DANCING, SLIDING AND AMAZING

Chickasaw Mudd Puppies included Beggar Weeds in their song "Florida."

"'Florida' is a song about a man that ran a junk store in the most David Lynchian state in the lower forty-eight. It was written while touring with the greatest Florida band that ever was, the Beggar Weeds from Jacksonville. It speaks to anyone that ever had the opportunity to play or see a show at the infamous Einstein A Go-Go and references the many mysteries that occurred on the sidewalks of Jax Beach."

— *Chickasaw Mudd Puppies*

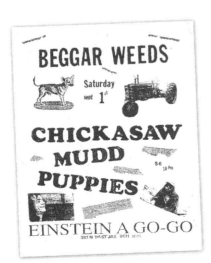

Scott Leuthold playing with Beggar Weeds, 1987

Adam Watson

Alan Cowart and Scott Leuthold

"Adam, Alan and I were happy with each other and rarely whined about driving and sleeping on floors. We shared most everything for six-and-a-half years and are connected for life."

— Scott Leuthold, BEGGAR WEEDS

CROWSDELL

Shannon Wright, Laurie Anne Wall and Paul Howell

"By opening this little punk club and their record stores, the Faircloths gave us so much. We were drifters and they brought us into their world of music and art. They gave us something to be exhilarated about, something to look forward to, something to burrow into, and maybe most importantly, a sanctum to be outsiders.

I met my Crowsdell bandmates at Einstein's. Our first show was opening up for local band Beggar Weeds. I really wanted Tammie to like us — she was obviously the coolest person in town. Although I was terribly shy and could barely move on stage, it was majestic to play Einstein's for the first time.

A few years later after we recorded our first 7-inch, I remember walking into Einstein's and seeing the dance floor full of kids dancing to our song. After growing up there, and seeing tons of bands, it was now our music that was being played through the speakers. It changed the course of my life forever."

— *Shannon Wright, CROWSDELL*

R o u n d o n e

CROWSDELL
WITH ~ SMOKE
(FORMER JODY GRINDERO AND FRIENDS FROM ATLANTA)

Saturday
April
-9-

Show stars at 9pm
$5.50 at the door

EINSTEIN
A GO GO

Steve Mason

BELL
BOOK
AND
CANDLE

James McCaffrey

"It's amazing how there was zero separation between the artists and the club kids. The kids were there because they loved the music and so did the bands. And the give and take, the back and forth was something I haven't seen since because most of the places now go out of their way to separate the audience from the performers."

— *James McCaffrey,*
Bell Book and Candle

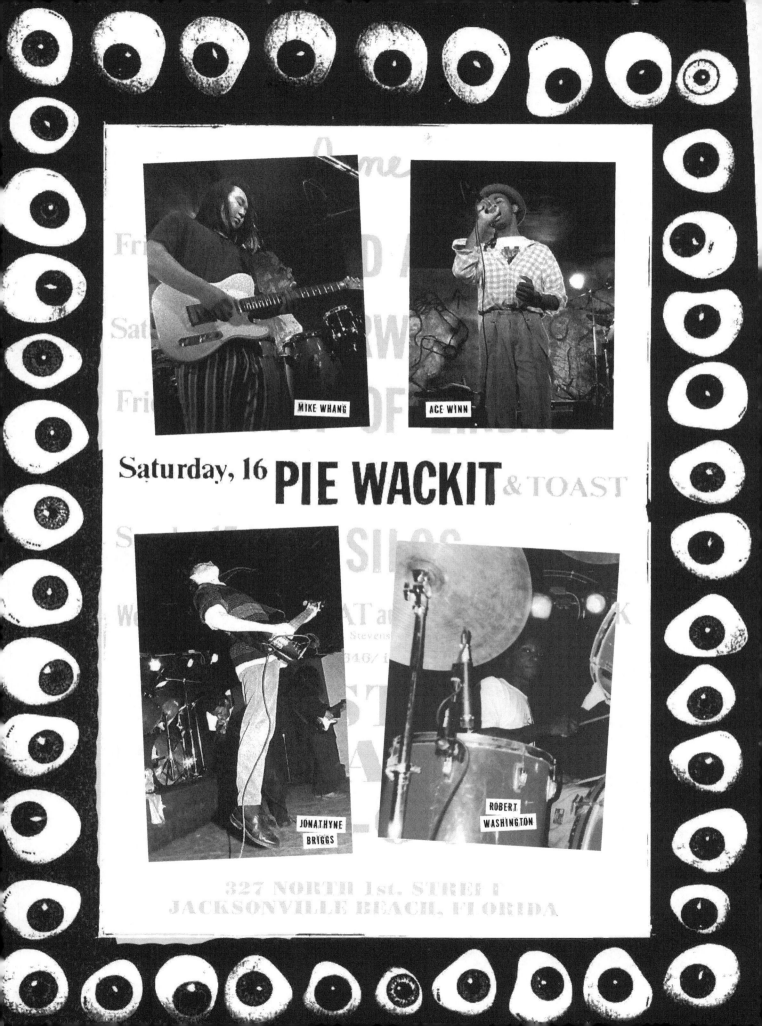

Saturday, 16 **PIE WACKIT** & TOAST

MIKE WHANG

ACE WINN

JONATHYNE BRIGGS

ROBERT WASHINGTON

327 NORTH 1st. STREET
JACKSONVILLE BEACH, FLORIDA

Mark Gentry and Ian Chase

REIN SANCTION

FRIDAY, DEC 22

A GOGO
JAX BCH 346-4072

Mark Gentry and Brannon Gentry

"Einstein A Go-Go was the focal point of our live performances for years. The mid- and late '80s music scene was stirring around the beach area but the Go-Go was where everyone felt free to be creative, including the dancing. Rein Sanction was always wanting a slot at Einstein's — as well as everyone else — for the chance to be heard. We were glad to have such a unique club to jam at and dance our way back to our parents' house by 1 a.m. Thank you to the Faircloth family for all the great years."

— *Brannon Gentry, REIN SANCTION*

COMMON THREAD

Joe Parker and Donald Kilpatrick (drums)

Travis Taylor

Joey Zimmerman

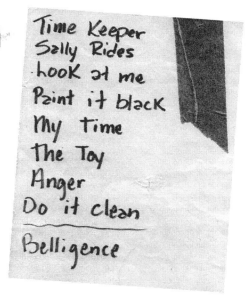

Time Keeper
Sally Rides
Look at me
Paint it black
My time
The Toy
Anger
Do it clean

Belligence

"Einstein's loomed large in our teen years. It was a big deal for us to play there the first time and was a special occasion every time after."
— JOE PARKER, *Common Thread*

common thread live at einstein a go-go WED. MAR. 14

YOU DON'T HAVE TO BE A STAR BABY... to come to this show!

COMMON THREAD vs. TODD JULY 17th EINSTEIN A GO-GO JAX. Beach

LOCAL SHOWCASE

"Einstein A Go-Go's importance in the local music scene cannot be overstated. It was a place where bands could be themselves, and the club's support of original music was instrumental in getting Jax's burgeoning alternative scene off the ground."
— *Steve Bauknecht, BIG VELVET ELVIS*

BiG Velvet Elvis

THURSDAY
July
2ND

CHRIS
GOOD-BYE
PARTY

Fender PRECISION BASS

Einstein A GoGo

SO WE'RE LOOKING FOR BASS PLAYERS

EINSTEIN A GO-GO
Presents

tintern abbey
and
FIN FANG FOOM
AUG. 2ND
8PM

lysergic garage party

"There weren't any college radio stations for me to learn about new music. The only outlet I had was *120 Minutes* on MTV and Einstein's. I learned about all these new bands that otherwise I probably would never have heard about and that shaped my tastes. It was a place where you could go down a rabbit hole and find all these great things that you like."
— *Eddie Sanchez, FIN FANG FOOM*

ROOM 136

UNDERGROUND MAN   *Pastis*

ROK

cadence faith

ITS PARTY TIME
STEVIE STILETTO
3 niGHTS
THURSDAY, AUG. 6TH —ENSTIEN A GOGO
(JAX. BCH.)
FRI. SAT., AUG 7TH + 8TH —POST AND KING LOUNGE
(RIVERSIDE)
The SPECIAL GUESTS
Mice

LAZZARRI

AVID
POLE

IN CONCERT AT
EINSTEIN A GO-GO

SALINE

WITH SELLA

WEDNESDAY, MARCH 30TH
AT 8:00 PM
$4.50 AT THE DOOR

NESTY BENEFIT CONCERT
from 6PM-11PM

featuring live music by:

★ **Jon Todd** ★
★ **Vishnu** ★
★ **The Cadets** ★
★ **Check Negative** ★
★ **Tintern Abbey** ★
★ **Lucidor** ★

Thursday Oct 24
$6.60

Doors open at 5PM
Open till 2AM with Dance Music

Einstein A Go-Go
327 N 1st St Jax Bch /call 249-4646 for info

...on Of The Proceeds Go To Amnesty International

CRAWFISH OF LOVE

NOMADIC ORPHANS

JULY 25TH   AT EINSTEIN A GO-GO

STRESS FEST

Pie Wackit   FEATURING   OUCH!
COMMON THREADS
TONY ROJAS

Wednesday, DEC 20th
STARTS AT 7PM · 4 BANDS · LOCALS OF COMEDY · DON'T BE LATE !!!

EINSTEIN A GO-GO
327 N 1ST St. · JAX BEACH

DAMP ENDING

PRESENTS

ASPLUNDH & **BELLE RIVE**

JUNE 11

asplundh

$4.50 COVER

ELLA MEGA LAST

EinsteinAGoGo

EVIL MARACAS

FORMERLY B.V.E.

JULY 29th

INNERSCARLET

REVOLVER

"I've said it before and I stand by it. No one fully appreciates the impact of the Faircloth family's passionate support of music in this town. When I was interviewed about Einstein's I pressed them to emphasize the Music Shops as infrastructure for more than just the 'scene.' They had Gary Starling teaching guitar in 1979 and a better LP section than the mall stores. I got my first cold call professional gig by having my info on their corkboard. I was just one of the knuckleheads who hung around there."

— *Crucial Eddy Cotton,*
PRETTY BOY FREUD

3 BLIND MICE

LOCAL SHOWCASE

STARK NAKED & **THE CAR THIEF**
WED 13 NOV

DOGSHOW INDIAN & **CRACKER SWAMP**
WED 20 NOV

LOST PROPHET
WED 27 NOV

ALL SHOWS $3

246-4073

FLAW   Peace Rhino

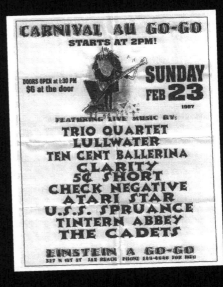

CARNIVAL AU GO-GO
STARTS AT 2PM!

DOORS OPEN at 1:30 PM
$6 at the door

SUNDAY FEB 23
1997

FEATURING LIVE MUSIC BY:

TRIO QUARTET
LULLWATER
TEN CENT BALLERINA
CLARITY
5¢ SHORT
CHECK NEGATIVE
ATARI STAR
U.S.S. SPRUANCE
TINTERN ABBEY
THE CADETS

EINSTEIN A GO-GO
327 N 1ST BY JAX BEACH   PHONE 249-4646 FOR INFO

"Before my first show, I was a complete wreck. I'm hanging out with Bill backstage because Bill was super chill and always made me feel comfortable. I was thinking this is going to fucking blow and I'm going to blow it when Bill said the show was going to be killer and a great time. I still wasn't convinced and he looks at me and he asks where I felt most comfortable playing my music. I said in my living room, so he suggested making the stage like my living room. 'Let's take this couch and put it up on the stage. Then we'll take that coffee table and a little lamp and we'll put it on the stage and it'll be just like your living room. We'll even put you an ashtray up there so you can smoke your cigarettes and you can even have a drink if you want.'" Really? Can we do that? Bill said we could and so we did. Actually, it did make me more relaxed, and I did have fun. It was way cooler than sitting up there on a stool."

— TONY ROJAS

Tony Rojas, 1989

Darren Ronan of Cotton Box

The Cadets were the very last band to play the club when it closed in 1997: Cash Carter, Chuck Smyth and Pete Cochrane

"Einstein A Go-Go was great because you could see and hear bands that were already successful and famous, bands that were about to be successful and famous, and bands that were never going to be successful or famous, all on the same stage. We never reached any real level of success, but every time we played there, for 45 minutes, it felt like we did. Every local band in town at that time felt the same way. "

— *Darren Ronan, COTTON BOX*

Cotton Box: Shane Myers, Darren Ronan, Heinrich (Doc) Kilgore and Buck, 1989

LIVE AT EINSTEIN A GO-GO

Gothic with Inferno

Wednesday
April 11
Doors Open 8:00
$2.00

Gothic and friends in the parking lot outside Einstein's, 1990

"I played with Inferno at Einstein's once, but played the metal bar next door, Peelers, many times. The turnout for our shows was usually mediocre. I remember going outside between sets and seeing what would seem like hundreds of kids buzzing in and out of Einstein's. There was a palpable energy coming from next door that almost made me resentful. What were we doing wrong? Why is all the buzz over there?"

— Paul Lapinski,
INFERNO, GUTBOY

"EAGG was many things for so many people. A place to dance and feel free. A venue for the best touring alternative bands of the '80s and '90s. A safe space for experimentation. A home for those who dared to stray from social norms. For me and so many other Jax musicians, it was also the place where we played our first shows. The Wednesday night Local Showcase provided us a real stage and a real sound system for our art, with few boundaries and no judgments. My first two bands played their first shows there, and I still geek out a bit thinking of how I got to play on the same stage as Nirvana, Jane's Addiction, The Replacements, et. al. Eternal thanks to the Faircloths for creating such a magical place."

— Brian Keele, *GOTHIC, LEE'A FAWL*

Bob Butterley and Brian Keele, 1990

LEE'A FAWL
UNPLUGGED

Wednesday,
June 5th, 1991
9 o'clock, $3.00

Einstein
A Go-Go
NORTH 'A' ST. JAX BEACH

Lee'a Fawl: Roger Butterley, Kenny Hamilton, Bob Butterley and Brian Keele, 1991

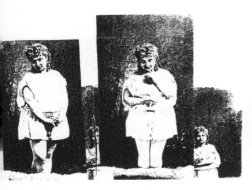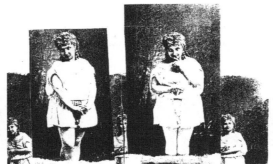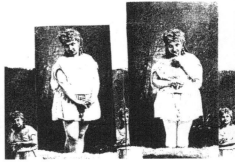

Saturday, Oct. 6
ALEKA'S ATTIC
(from Gainesville)

Tim Hankins

Josh McKay and River Phoenix

Rain Phoenix   River Phoenix

"I remember Einstein A Go-Go. It gave my teen self a sense of belonging in the local northeast Florida music scene and — added bonus, it was only blocks from the beach! It was a favorite stop for Aleka's Attic as we made our way up the East Coast on tour. A true original music venue that felt like a brick-and-mortar 'zine."

— *Rain Phoenix*, Aleka's Attic

"Aleka's Attic always drew a large crowd because River Phoenix was a big movie star at the time. I'd cook vegan food like tofu vegetable stir fry for the rest of the band who were all very friendly and would hang out before the show. I didn't interact much with River or his sister Rain though their mother would be there, and River and his girlfriend at the time, Martha Plimpton, would show up right before the show. Because music came before his acting, he always seemed much more than his teen heartthrob image."

— MARIANNA WHANG

Mitch Easter and Janine Cooper

Angie Carlson and Mitch Easter

John Heames

Mitch Easter and John Heames

"Einstein's was just a really friendly place. A lot of clubs are just rough physically, and this place was really comfortable. It had that family and friendly vibe about it. The whole hospitality thing was great. When we played it was a really good show because it was an all-ages club and that was just wonderful because most places weren't. It was just great to play for kids and they were super into it.

The first time I saw a CD of our music was at Einstein's. Some kid was out on the street and wanted us to sign it."

— MITCH EASTER, *Let's Active*

THE MUSIC SHOP PRESENTS:

LET'S ACTIVE

Nº 95

pip tickets

WEDNESDAY, SEPTEMBER 2½

EINSTEIN A GO-GO
327 N. 1st ST., JAX. BCH.

LET'S ACTIVE

SATURDAY, DECEMBER 30th

10:30 p.m. $9.00

Nº 178

Angie Carlson

The Connells

SATURDAY, JULY 8

EINSTEIN A GO-GO
327 N. 1st. JAX. BCH, FL. 32250
249-4646

Doug MacMillan

David Connell

George Huntley

Mike Connell

THE EXCEPTION

IT WAS A GRIND PACKING six guys into a van along with equipment. There were plenty of nights that we would not get a hotel room and just slept as best we could in the van. Then when we could afford a hotel room it was six guys in one room, and we were not eating well and drinking too much. So, the moments when we were actually playing and the show was going well, we were reminded of why we started doing it in the first place.

So many clubs and venues were just so impersonal, and you would go and bide your time until you had to play and to varying degrees of wretchedness. Then there were those few venues like Einstein's that were the exception. The Faircloths made it so clear that it was the bands that mattered. And of course, they had maybe the best fried chicken I've ever had in my life.

— MIKE CONNELL,
The Connells

Peele Wimberley

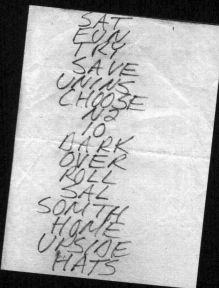

EINSTEIN A GO - GO PRESENTS;
THE CONNELLS
WITH EIGHT OR NINE FEET
SATURDAY, JULY 8 $6

Saturday · July 8TH ... The CONNELLS

George Huntley (signature)

"We played as the connells for the first time in September of 1984, which was the start of my third year of law school. I thought I would finish law school, take the bar and be a lawyer. But by May of '85 things were going better than any of us had expected. We had 10 tunes by that point, which was getting the critical mass where you could record an album, and just followed where that went. We didn't have a vision or the work ethic that a lot of bands have. We were really lucky that people responded to whatever it was we were doing, and were genereous to us."

— MIKE CONNELL, *The Connells*

TRY
F&G
INSIDE
CHOOSE
ELEGANCE
10 PINS   UNINSPIRED
OVER   IF IT CR
(HEY WOW)   DARK D
NEW   SAT
I SUPPOSE
HOME
UPSIDE
SCOTTY
SAL
SOMETHING

The Theory Shop Presents;

POLVO

IN CONCERT

Saturday, March **4** 1995 10:15 PM

$5.50

Einstein A Go-Go 327 N 1st St Jax Bch

16556/JR

Polvo Tour Rider

This rider is hereby agreed to be attached to, and thereby making it an integral part of the original engagement contract entered between _T maclur_ (hereafter referred to as "the promoter") and I.C.M. (hereafter referred to as "The Agent") for a performance by the musical act known as Polvo on the date of _4/8/96_ by both principal parties of that contract, the promoter and the agent. Any and all terms made by this rider both amend and supersede any similar or like ones presented in the original engagement contract that are not included in this rider are still considered binding. The Terms of this Rider are:

1) The promoter agrees to furnish at his/her expense all that is necessary for the presentation of Polvo such requirements shall follow.

2) Polvo shall have sole and exclusive control over the presentation and performance of the engagement hereunder. The obligations of Polvo hereunder are subject to detention or prevention by sickness, inability to perform, accident, means of transportation, Acts of God, riots, labor difficulties, any act or order of any public authority or any cause, similar or dissimilar, beyond the control of Polvo.

3) The promoter agrees to provide a top quality PA system and monitor system with three discrete mixes (vocal, drums, guitar - side) and four wedges.

4) The promoter agrees to provide one clean room to accommodate band members and their crew. With the dressing room, the promoter will provide: meals for four people or money to buy such meals,($ 8 a head Buy-Out) 1 case of imported beer, 2 quarts of orange juice, 5 one liter bottles of non-carbonated mineral water. Ample and continual supply of Fresh Coffee and Tea. (**+ 4 Large clean Towels and (2) Duracell Nine Volt Batteries)**

5) Polvo shall have the sole and exclusive right, but not obligation, to sell souvenir items, including T-shirts, records and tapes, etc.., in connection with the performance hereunder and the receipts thereof shall belong exclusively to Polvo. The promoter agrees to provide an area inside the venue so the artist or its associates can sell merchandise if they so desire.

6) The promoter guarantees proper security at all times to insure the safety of the band, crew, their instruments, equipment, and personal property before, during, and after the show.

7) Polvo shall receive billing in 100% type in all advertising and publicity issued or under the control of the promoter in regard to the engagement hereunder. 75 % Special Guest billing in support situations

All inquiries regarding promotional material should be directed to :

Merge Records P.O. Box 1235 Chapel Hill, NC 27514 (919) 929-0711	Touch And Go Records P.O. Box 25520 Chicago, IL. 60625 (312) 463-8316

Promoter _____ date _____

Agent _____ dat _____

"The first time I saw Sebadoh at EAGG I interviewed Lou Barlow for my high school newspaper. I said, 'Hey, you know Polvo is playing here next week' and Lou said, 'No way,' went to the green room and wrote on the wall 'Polvo I ♡ you, Lou... B....' Later, when they were disassembling Einstein's, my friend Andrew Bowers cut that section out with a hacksaw and framed it for it me."

— DANIEL GILL

THINKING FELLERS UNION LOCAL #282 & **POLVO**
SUNDAY MAY 19 9PM $8
EINSTEIN A GO-GO

FETCHIN BONES

CLAY RICHARDSON

HOPE NICHOLLS

To the BEST CLUB IN THE USA: Einstein A Go Go!

FETCHIN BONES

"Einstein's was like the best dance party and the best rock 'n' roll. The DJing there was always great. I remember the first time I ever heard The Sugarcubes I was dancing on that dance floor after we played a show. And I was like 'What the hell is this? It was 'Birthday.'' It was an iconic moment for me."

— HOPE NICHOLLS, *Fetchin Bones*

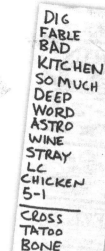

```
HOUSE          DIG
THINGS         FABLE
FABLE          BAD
SAMMY          KITCHEN
EXIT           SO MUCH
BIND           DEEP
YOU THIRST     WORD
LENA           ASTRO
KITCHEN        WINE
PLUS 7         STRAY
WINE           LC
RIDING         CHICKEN
STRAY          5-1
BED            ─────
CHICKEN        CROSS
BRIEFCASE      TATOO
─────          BONE
STEAM          ─────
SUPER          SOBRILL
SO BRILL       MY
─────
JESSE
KINGDOM
3 FOOT 2
```

ERROL
STEWART

DANNA
PENTES

"It was such a great location. You could walk around the beach after the soundcheck. It's great to play a place where you feel appreciated and it was always packed."

— ERROL STEWART, *Fetchin Bones*

AARON
PITKIN

"It didn't feel like there was a barrier between the stage and the audience and there's something about the energy in a situation like that. So, it was the connection as well. The all-ages aspect made for a different feeling in the club because it was less of a bar scene and people came more for the music and to be involved in the process."

—*Danna Pentes*, *Fetchin Bones*

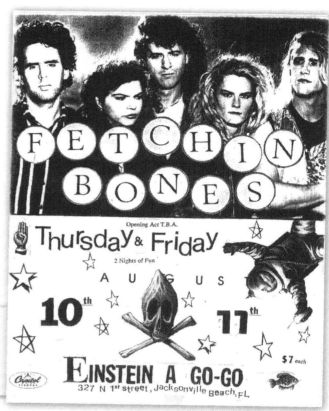

"The first time we played there Bill [Faircloth] was in the back making red beans and rice. He had this hat that was for some landscaping place and he gave it to me."

— ERROL STEWART, *Fetchin Bones*

"I was a huge fanboy! I think I proposed to Hope from the audience once."

— Robert Cooper

"We never had a vision for a sound. I do recall when my sister told me about The B-52's and I listened to it and I'm like, 'OK, I can sing like this.' I felt like the energy and the creativity being more important than virtuosity. That was always a guide for me. Just do what you love creatively and hopefully somebody else is going to love it. But what else is there to do? We were never in it for the money or to try to be like other people. It was all about self-expression and if it makes you happy, hopefully it makes some other people happy."

— *Hope Nicholls, Fetchin Bones*

"I don't even know how many times I saw them there, but every single show was ridiculous fun."

— *Julie Morris*

"We loved Einstein's because it was not just frat kids or any one group. It was a great, diverse mix of people. And that's a beautiful thing."

— *Hope Nicholls, FETCHIN BONES*

Fetchin Bones, 1988

"Einstein A Go-Go was one of the few venues The dB's were booked to play in Florida. Tammie and Terri were great hosts. We did a swell show and then they took us over a chain link fence to go swimming, which just added to our fun evening."

— *Peter Holsapple,* The dB's

Will Rigby, Peter Holsapple and Eric Peterson

Peter Holsapple

SATURDAY, MARCH 19 $8

Einstein a Go Go 327 n 1st st, jax bch
249 4646

98

"Before we went to Einstein's, It was presented as 'Oh, we got you a gig at Einstein's and you're gonna love it. It's unlike any other place you're going to play on this tour. It's gonna be comfortable. They're gonna treat you well. The crowd is going to be awesome because they're going to be kids who want to be there not getting drunk. They're going to be into hearing you.' And, you know, that was our experience.

The club was singular. It was so unique. The tone of it was unlike any other place. And we loved that it was on a beach. That was pretty neat. I can remember running out after the show and into the water. The club didn't serve alcohol, but we drank plenty of beer."

— JIM WILBUR, *Superchunk*

Laura Ballance and Mac McCaughan

Seed Toss
Skip Steps
30 Xtra
Cast Iron
SLACK
Binding
Tie A Rope
Sick to Me
cool
Spring A Leak
Punch Me Harder
For Tension
the Breadman
Throwing Things

"Mac McCaughan and I were sitting at the bar by the front door before the club opened talking about old punk music. So I asked him who his favorite Black Flag singer was and he said 'Dez.' I said 'no way, Rollins was way better.' The two of us just went back and forth over who was the better singer of Black Flag."

— *Sonny Thigpen*

"I remember someone was smoking weed in the audience and Mac from Superchunk looked into the crowd and was like, 'Alright, who's got the doobage?' My friends and I routinely asked each other that in our best high-pitched Mac voice for years after that. Also, the crowd definitely slam danced at that show, egged on by the band. Laura from Superchunk said 'we're seeing some great dancing out there. This next one's called 'Punch Me Harder,' which really got the dancers excited."

— *Justin Ebert*

In Concert Tuesday Dec 6, 1994

ARCHERS OF LOAF

9:30PM $5.00

E i n s t e i n A G O - G O
327 N 1st St Jacksonville Beach 249-4646

No. 228

ARCHERS of LOAF

Photo: Michael Levine

"One time when
Archers of Loaf
played, Tammie had
me be their servant
boy. Whatever they
needed I got. It
was incredible
because I'm a
huge fan and I
got to hang out
with them."

— Bryan Massey

"There would be bands that you thought of as rock stars, but
they didn't think of themselves as rock stars like Archers of Loaf.
They came through, the show was sold out and they couldn't believe it."
— *Chris Gibson, THE JULIUS AIRWAVE*

FLAT DUO JETS

SATURDAY · MAY 25
10:30 PM   FIVE DOLLARS

Einstein A Go-Go
327 N 1st St. Jax Bch (Ph) 249-4646

RE: Flat Duo Jets
May 1, 1994
Jacksonville Beach, FL
Einstein A Go-Go

Dear Tammy :
Enclosed please find the Contracts and Riders for the above referenced
engagement. Please sign all Contracts and Riders and return them
with the appropriate deposit no later than **April 20, 1994**.
Please note that the amount of the deposit due is **$125.00**. A fully
executed Contract and Rider will be returned to you for your records.

DEPOSIT INFORMATION

All deposits must be in the form of a U.S. Money Order, Certified Check or
Cashiers Check made payable to Electric Artists in U.S. Currency.
WE DO NOT ACCEPT PERSONAL OR COMPANY CHECKS.

Best of luck for a successful show. If you have any questions,
please do not hesitate to call.

Kindest regards,

Andrea Webb
/ Electric Artists

Daniel Chavis

Joe Boyle

THE VELDT

Danny C. Chavis

"The club was full of young kids eager to hear new music (or 'alternative' as they called it). The atmosphere was electric. We opened for Fetchin Bones who was big on the *CMJ* charts. I remember we had a seafood feast for dinner and the family was more than accommodating. It was a magical time."

— *Danny C. Chavis, THE VELDT*

THE NICEST
BUNCH OF FOLKS

PLAYING EINSTEIN'S WAS my first-ever out-of-town gig. And, it was my first show with Mr. Crowe's Garden, which became The Black Crowes. We literally said "this is the greatest night ever. We'll be back as often as they'll have us." And we never went back. It was the only time we ever played there, to my eternal regret. I mean that not just because it was so special to me to play a gig in a foreign land, but because we were never treated as well again. It was really the nicest bunch of folks ever. We had such a blast. And that gig was special, not just to me, but to the Robinson brothers. We talked about that gig for years. It was really special to all of us.

I'm in a town where I don't know anybody, we're gonna get maybe 50 bucks. You know, we were getting gas money to get two cars there and back. But what I didn't understand until that night, there's this whole network of clubs that are run by really cool people, and they're very supportive. Three of us stayed overnight and slept in the club because they let us crash there. The next day we met the Beggar Weeds and they were our tour guides for the day. The Long Ryders played the following night. They turned up and they were great. We said, "We played here last night and stayed over to see you," and they invited us to hang out. Their tour manager was a great guy and he ended up working for The Black Crowes three years later. We had a record out and were on a big tour when he walked into the dressing room and we were like, "We met you at Einstein's three years ago. Holy shit!"

—STEVE GORMAN, *Mister Crowe's Garden/The Black Crowes*

JOPE · MARY MY HOPE · MARY MY HOPE

Sven Pipien

James Hall

Clinton Steele

SATURDAY JAN. 24TH ~ KILKENNY CATS ON TWIN TONE RECORD

"We had some really awesome times there. One of the things I remember — besides the fact that they were welcoming and treated the bands well — the fans were always great. We always had good crowds and lots of fun. We would try to get there early because the guitarist and I liked to play on the beach. So, we would be out there building sand castles and stuff until the bitter end. We tried to do as much of that as possible before we went in and got ready for the show. It was so much fun."

— **Tom Cheek,** *Kilkenny Cats*

saturday, june 20

KILKENNY CATS

from Athens, GA

EINSTEIN A GOGO
327 N 1st ST JAX BCH

Tom Cheek

Sean O'Brien

Keith Landers

"There was college radio back then and that was an indie/alternative sound, but it wasn't defined yet. And then there was all that sort of new wave stuff that was starting to break in the mainstream. But the college radio stuff was underground, like Hüsker Dü, Mission of Burma, The Replacements, R.E.M., and a lot of American bands. They cut their teeth in these college towns and they got their exposure on college radio."

— TOM CHEEK, *Kilkenny Cats*

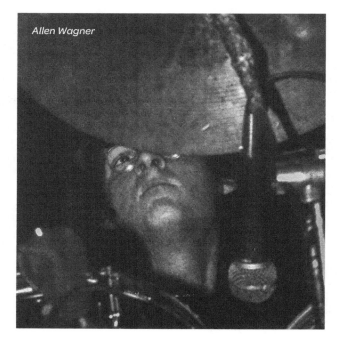

Allen Wagner

HETCH HETCHY

Ian Chase, Lynda Stipe and Andrew Brown

Lynda Stipe

Take heed, go, prophet
Say now, quietly, all
Say now, 6 still
Prophet plays a game w/ clocks
I am the rogue against him

I feel the noise against him
I hear the beat " "
I am the hell below him now
His servants, all against him
I saw them when they
    danced in
Here are the words against
    him now

Take the river in a one inch
    measure
Wrap it up only in leisure
Take an inch out

"Jeff Totty and I made the trip from Gainesville to Einstein's to see Hetch Hetchy. Jeff warned me that the show would likely be different than anything we'd seen before. While Hetch Hetchy had a 4AD sound, they also had a unique stage presence, with Jay shirtless, crouching, and making animal sounds, and Lynda's soaring vocals. I really loved the song 'Present' but couldn't decipher all the lyrics. After the show, I approached Lynda and asked what two of the lines were, and she said, 'Hold on, I'll write the lyrics down for you' and she jotted them on a scrap of paper — which was incredibly kind — as several people had lined up to meet her."

— *Siobhan White*

HETCH HETCHY
Saturday, March 5
EINSTEIN
A GO-GO

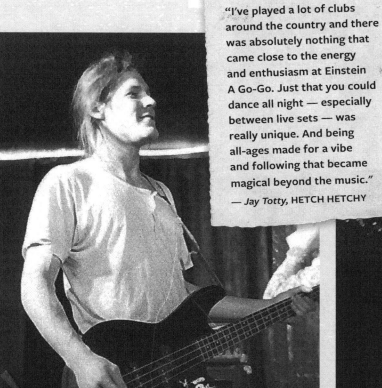

> "I've played a lot of clubs around the country and there was absolutely nothing that came close to the energy and enthusiasm at Einstein A Go-Go. Just that you could dance all night — especially between live sets — was really unique. And being all-ages made for a vibe and following that became magical beyond the music."
> — *Jay Totty*, HETCH HETCHY

Clockwise from top left: Jay Totty, Andrew Brown, Ian Chase and Rene Garcia

DREAMS SO REAL

FEATURED IN ATHENS INSIDE AND OUT

Barry Marler

Trent Allen

CHickasaw mudd puppies

From ATHENS, GA

MR. SHORTY
NIGHT
CICADA
LON
FROGMORE
FLATCAR
BILL
NOTHIN
RAVEN
SUPER
SHANNON
DO YOU
WASP

WASH
WORDS

Brant Slay

Jeff Walls

Murray Attaway

GUADALCANAL DIARY

John Poe

Rhett Crowe

CHOMPFISH

Chompfish: James Shinholser, Russ Kennington and Jance Brown, 1987

drivin' n' cryin'

Kevn Kinney and Tim Nielsen, 1987

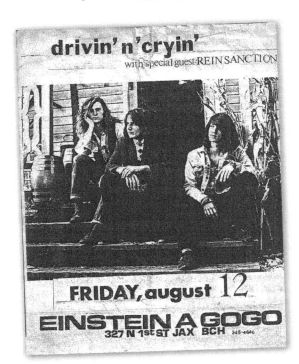

drivin' n' cryin'
with special guest REIN SANCTION

FRIDAY, august 12
EINSTEIN A GOGO
327 N 1ST ST JAX BCH 245-4646

"When we played at Einstein's they would make us food and give us a cooler with an allotment of beer. But once we were driving from Atlanta, we hit traffic and missed soundcheck. We pretty much had to go on right after the opening act. Bill was pissed so he sat on our cooler and wouldn't let us have our beer until after the show. I was just sorry I missed the fried chicken."

— *Kevn Kinney, Drivin N Cryin*

Amy Ray and Emily Saliers, 1987

INDIGO GIRLS

FROM ATLANTA FOUR DOLLARS

"I bought the first Indigo Girls EP at the Theory Shop. Then years later, I got Amy and Emily to autograph it, and they're like, 'Where the hell did you get this? We don't even have a copy of this.'"

— Jim Leatherman

friday, june 19 INDIGO GIRLS FROM ATLANTA

saturday june 20
KILKENNY CATS

FEATURED IN ATHENS GA
— INSIDE OUT

A
MUSIC
SHOP
PRODUCTION

EINSTEIN A GOGO
EINSTEIN A GOGO
EINSTEIN A GOGO
327 N 1st ST JAX BCH 246-4075
249-4646

PYLON

10:30 pm $7 TICKETS ON SALE

EVERYTHING IS COOL

Vanessa Briscoe Hay, Curtis Crowe (drums), Michael Lachowski and Randall Bewley, 1989

"Einstein A Go-Go was very unique for the time and the kids really got what they wanted there as far as seeing bands. They had incredible credibility with the independent music community.

It was a really neat place. I liked the fact that it was all ages and it was also one of the few clubs in Florida with a mix of different races. I remember there was no alcohol and the kids were just dancing. We got to experience playing a show to a sober audience without anyone yelling 'Free Bird.'"

— VANESSA BRISCOE HAY, *Pylon*

"Pylon was the band that altered my teen microcosm brain. It was after seeing them play that I decided I was going to be a musician. The singer Vanessa was unlike anyone else. She had this unstoppable urgency that was like a sea of sparks, illuminating each of her steps on stage."
— *Shannon Wright,* *Crowsdell*

Michael Lachowski and Randall Bewley

CRAZY
COOL
WORK
GRAV
SPRING
THERE IT IS
REP
CATCH
LAKE
IMT
THIS THAT
DANGER
CHUG
NO CLOX
B-COMP.
K
BEEP
VOLUME
FEAST
—
M-TRAIN
JACK
STOP
—
SLOGAN
BUZZ

"I don't remember anything about the bathrooms so that probably means they were clean."
— Vanessa Briscoe Hay, PYLON

Vanessa Briscoe Hay

FAITH NO MORE

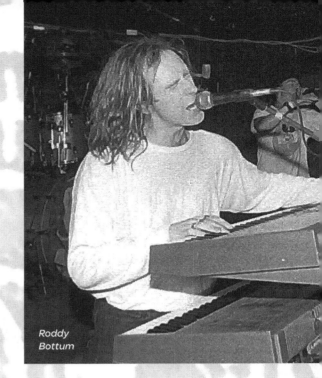

Roddy
Bottum

Billy Gould and Mike Patton

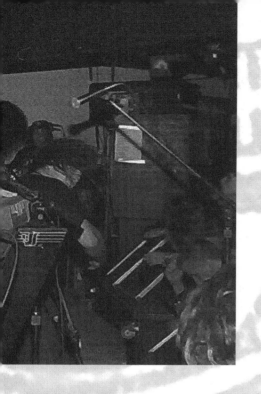

Jim Martin

Mike Bordin

It's back to the beach...

fish bone

on columbia records

Hey, they partied with Annette

$8.00
AT THE DOOR

THURSDAY
NOV. 19TH
SHOWTIME 9 PM

EINSTEIN A GO-GO
327 N. 1ST ST. JAX BCH (PH) 249-4646 FOR INFO

*Angelo Moore
of Fishbone, 1987*

Norwood Fisher

Kendall Jones

Philip "Fish" Fisher

Walter A. Kibby II

RED HOT CHILI PEPPERS

WED, DEC 2

9pm

with special guest; FAITH NO MORE $12

EINSTEIN A GOGO

327 N 1st ST JAX BCH   246-4073
                                                          249-4646

"Being at a height disadvantage, standing in front of speakers was the only place I could see the band. Please tell the Chili Peppers that they owe me some hearing aids."

— Betsie Green

"The Red Hot Chili Peppers show was sold out and the fire marshal had constraints about the number of people in the club and how late the show could go. Tammie came to me in the DJ booth and told me that when they're done to thank everybody and drop the needle on a record because the fire marshal was here and we had to close. They played their last song and the Chili Peppers were fucking on fire. You're not going to tell them not to play an encore, so I said, 'Thanks everyone for coming out,' and put on the lamest song ever. The place goes absolutely berserk. Tammie runs up to me and says, 'What are you doing?!' So I took the needle off and the band comes back onstage. Every single member of the Red Hot Chili Peppers flipped me off on the way to the stage."

— IAN CHASE, *Rein Sanction*

sunday
NOV. 1st
10 pm
$12

X

EXENE CERVENKA   JOHN DOE   TONY GILKYSON   D.J. BONEBRAKE

TO EINSTEIN
A-GO-GO
Best of Luck
John D

AFTER HOURS

I WORKED THE BAR THE NIGHT THAT X played. In the band lounge I saw Exene Cervenka and Gigi Blair (John Doe's wife) wrap their very pregnant bellies with towels to protect the babies from soundwaves. A lot of older people were there to see the show and I often had to explain that Einstein's was a non-alcoholic club.

The show was sold out and then some. People sat on the counter so I only got glimpses between the fans blocking my view. There were long vertical beams of glowing orange stage lights and sometimes John Doe drifted by. But one does not go to see X. You go to hear them. X rode the wave of their musical groove that night in fantastic glory. The music seemed to envelop me. I'd never heard harmonies like that before and it may have been the most polished show I ever saw, or rather, heard.

After the club closed the band did one of my favorite things a band could do — they hung out with us. Exene and Gigi sat with their feet up enjoying a second dinner. Exene's husband, Viggo Mortensen, (yes, "Aragorn" of *Lord of the Rings* fame) was there. John Doe commented on one of the Gibson guitar bar stools Bill Faircloth had refurbished, admiring the care and work he had put into the job. Bill said, "You can have it. I know you'll give it a good home." John was visibly taken back. He needed a moment before he said, "Man, that is the nicest thing anyone's done." Then they hugged.

— *Allison Durham*

Henry Rollins, 1986

EINSTEIN A GO-GO PRESENTS:

AN EVENING WITH...

HENRY ROLLINS

CALL 246-4073 FOR INFO

TAMMY, THANKS FOR THE SHOW.
— HENRY

ARTWORK RAYMOND PETTIBON ©SST PUBS

ROLLINS BOOKING INFO:

ROLLINS / 2-13-61
PO BOX 2461
REDONDO BEACH, CA
90278 - USA

THE GOOD GUYS: IAN MacKAYE, JILL HEATH, BLACK FLAG, GREG GINN, BILL STEVENSON, KIRA ROESSLER, CHUCK DUKOWSKI, SPOT, JOE, MUGGER, DAVO, SST BANDS, BAD BRAINS, HARVEY KUBERNIK, TOM DOO, IRIS & LES, NICK CAVE, DEIRDRE O'DONOGHUE, LYDIA LUNCH, ALEC, JCK BRWR, X, DANZIG, MIKE, SIMON, WENDEL, SKIP, H.R., RATMAN, MR. RICK SPELLMAN (TATTOOS), MARCY, JESSAMY, STACI ROLFE; THE GINNS, RAYMOND PETTIBON, JULIE, LYDIA E. ADAMS, M.A., H. MILLER, C.M.M., JON LIU, KCRW F.M., COFFEE ACHIEVERS EVERYWHERE.

FIRST PRESSING, NUMBER ___144___ OF 1,000
H44

2

TWO THIRTEEN SIXTY ONE
HENRY ROLLINS

"YES YES WITH A BIG SOUL"
— JOHN LEE HOOKER

— HENRY H/H
2-13-61

GOING GLOBAL

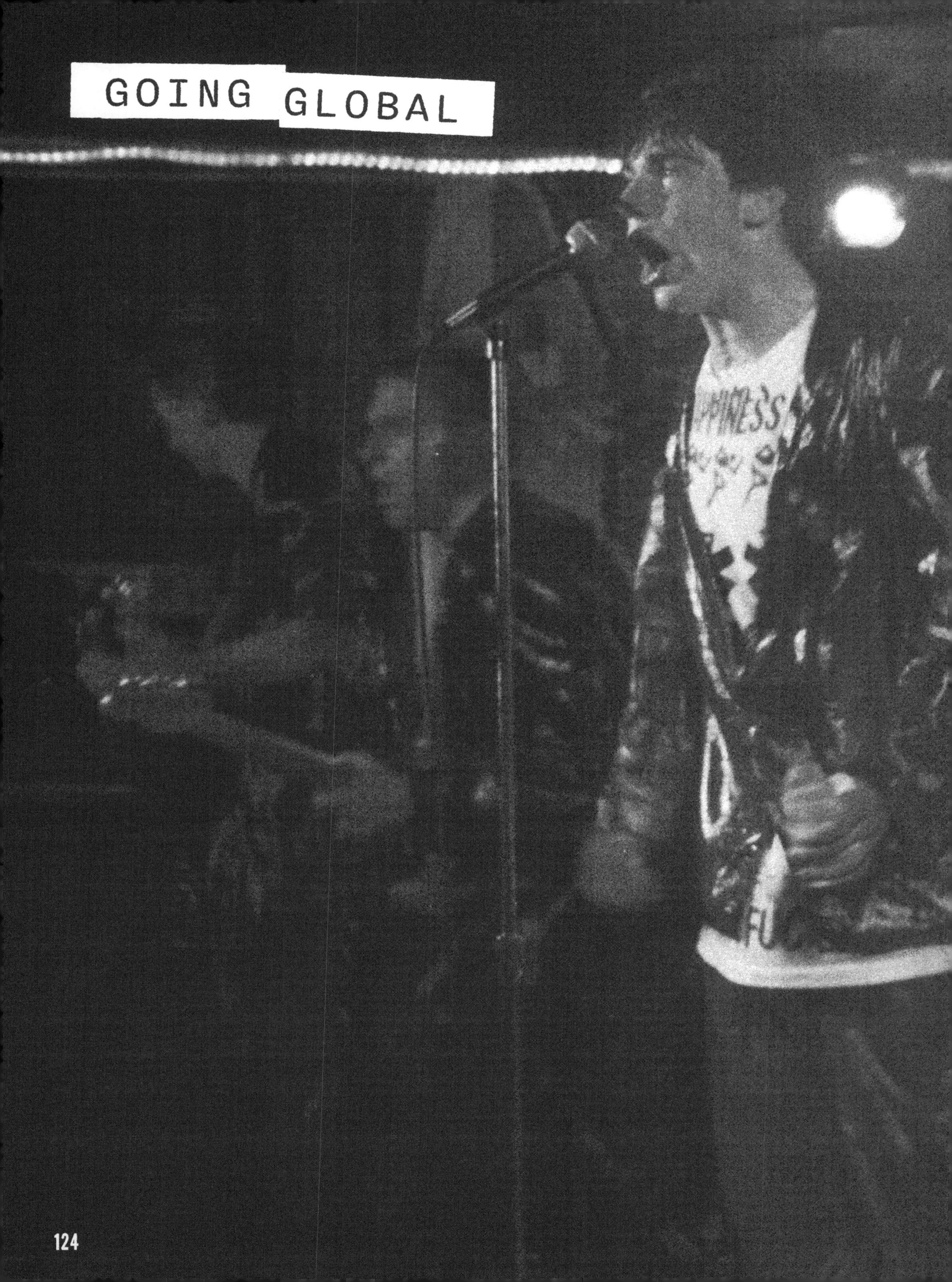

Martin Atkins and
Margot Olavarria of
Brian Brain, 1988

NEW MODEL ARMY

SUNDAY, AUG. 2

Jason Harris   Slade the Leveller   Robb Heston

FROM ENGLAND

EINSTEIN A GOGO
327 N 1st ST JAX BCH   246-4073
249-4646

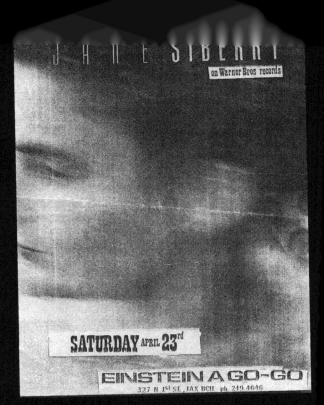

JANE SIBERRY
on Warner Bros records

SATURDAY APRIL 23rd

EINSTEIN A GO-GO
327 N 1st ST. JAX BCH. ph 249 4646

"My first EAGG show was Jane Siberry, spring
of 1988. In between songs this dude was
screaming 'Rebecca!' I think one of her backup
singers was named Rebecca. After several
minutes of this, Jane said something like 'We
are all Rebecca tonight,' and kind of laughed.
I think the guy was finally escorted out."

— Tom Hartwell

FUN WITH MUSIC !

BRIAN BRAIN

thursday, march 31

EINSTEIN A GO-GO
327 N 1st ST. JAX BCH ph 249 4646

THE SAINTS

WITH SPECIAL GUEST:
BIG DIPPER

ON TVT RECORDS

from Australia

SATURDAY, OCT 24 $6

THE MUSIC SHOP PRESENTS:
MODERN ENGLISH
MARCH 29, SATURDAY
EINSTEIN A-GO-GO
327 N. 1st ST., JAX BCH

pip tickets ®

SIX DOLLARS

∞

No:

"Modern English played the most fucked up and amazing version of 'Life in the Gladhouse' that I've ever heard." —James McCaffrey

Robbie Grey

DON'T MISS SPRING B

SATURDAY MARCH **22**

WEDNESDAY MARCH **26**

THURSDAY MARCH **27**

SATURDAY MARCH **29**

SHOW STARTS AT 10

MODERN ENGLISH

ON SIRE RECORDS

APRIL 4, FRIDAY - TRYCYCLE THIEVES • SAT. APRIL 5 - LOVE TRACTOR
FRIDAY APRIL 11 - THE SILO'S • SATURDAY APRIL 12 - FETCHIN BONES

EINSTEIN A-GO-GO
327 N. 1st. ST, JAX BCH
PH) 246-4073 FOR INFO

CALL 246-4073 FOR TICKET PRICE

THE NIGHT MOM SHOWED UP AT EINSTEIN'S

MOJO NIXON

tickets on sale now $12 9:30pm

Sunday, March 10

EINSTEIN A GO GO

327 N. 1st ST. , Jacksonville Beach
phone 246-4073 / 249-4646

"Venture Booking and Frank Riley booked us at Einstein A Go-Go, like they did for Fetchin Bones and Pylon. I remember we went to the club, met the sisters, along with their parents, and they were making food for us! We were happy to eat anything that wasn't barbecue or Waffle House."

— *Mojo Nixon*

IT WAS AN ALL-AGES DEAL SO there were a lot of kids — by kids I mean people under 25. Me and Skid are playing, we're doing our show and it's going well. I'm telling my jokes, everybody's laughing and whatnot. Then halfway through the show there's a commotion in the back of the room. I can't tell what's going on but somebody's obviously angry. It's a mother of one of the kids who was down front, and like a cartoon she has on a pink housecoat and pink curlers in her hair. So she obviously got ready to go to bed and found out her daughter snuck out and is at the rock 'n' roll club with the Mojo Nixon and demons and the devil. The mom is screaming like some kind of crazy hillbilly. The first thing she does is she knocks the clove cigarette out of her daughter's mouth and comments on her black eye makeup. Mom grabs her daughter by the collar and drags her out of the club. I've stopped. I'm not even playing anymore and all the kids are afraid their moms are coming next.

— MOJO NIXON

MOJO NIXON & SKID ROPER

Tuesday, april 19 9pm $6

EINSTEIN A GO GO 327 N 1st ST, JAX BEACH

No. 37

"At some point in the late '80s I caught Mojo Nixon at Einstein A Go-Go in Jacksonville. Some drunk next to me was heckling and causing trouble and ended up bumping into me. A couple shoves later and the guy took a swing at me, so I knocked him down. As he starts to get up Mojo jumps off the stage midsong, points a finger in the guy's face, yells 'STAY DOWN,' then hops back up and keeps playing, not missing a beat. The guy was suitably chastened and well behaved throughout the remainder of the performance. After the set I helped Mojo kill a case of Busch backstage while we talked about Otis Redding and our favorite soul singers. I was maybe 18. RIP Mojo, you had some funny damn songs, but you were a real one through and through."

— Pat Hughes

SATURDAY, july 28...

GLASS EYE

Sunday, july 30

MOJO NIXON & SKID ROPER

EINSTEIN A GO-GO
327 N 1st street, Jacksonville Beach, FL

Ph 246-4073
249-4646

"We knew that Mojo was pretty wild so combine 'wild' with 'boredom' and two art students. We sat down and used black Sharpies to do the shirts. Connie let us in early and we turned into Mojo magnets. Mojo said 'Not only are y'all fine and devoted, YOU'RE INSANE!' He literally yelled it!"

— NATASHA WEIMANN (with KELLY BRYANT)

"I lived in Atlantic Beach and we always had something going on at my house. I hung around musicians, skaters and surfers so having a rock band stay over was not out of the norm. Man or Astroman? stayed one night and woke up early. They felt awkward because they didn't know where I'd taken them. My mom got up and found Coco the Electronic Monkey Wizard and Birdstuff poking around and offered them breakfast. She had the mixer going and bacon ready before they knew it and the rest of the guys joined them at the table. I came down about an hour later to find everyone in the dining room and kitchen. Our family still laughs about it.

At their second show I was invited to dance with the Mexican wrestler's mask and when I went up on stage a fight broke out at the door. Tammie Faircloth and Sonny Thigpen broke it up, but the crowd was fully focused on the ruckus. My moment to shine was stolen by fight-thirsty bandicoots."

— ALAN GREY

WARNING: ALL EARTHLINGS..

Friday, May 6th

IN CONCERT

MAN OR ASTROMAN

$6.00 AT THE DOOR
SHOW STARTS AT 10PM
CALL 249-4646 FOR INFO

AT YOUR FAVORITE EARTH STATION:

EINSTEIN A GO-GO
327 N. 1st Street
Jacksonville Beach, Florida   Earth

Star Crunch and Coco the Electronic Monkey Wizard, 1994

NOW EXPLOSION

Lahoma van Zandt

Elouise "Champagne" Montague Mellencamp

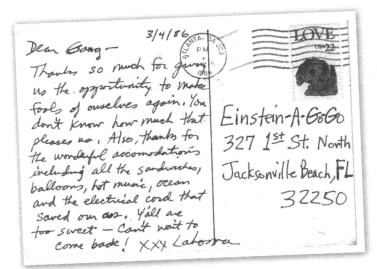

Dear Gang—
Thanks so much for giving
us the opportunity to make
fools of ourselves again. You
don't know how much that
pleases us. Also, thanks for
the wonderful accommodations
including all the sandwiches,
balloons, hot music, ocean
and the electrical cord that
saved our ass. Y'all are
too sweet — Can't wait to
come back! XXX Lahoma

3/4/86

Einstein·A·GoGo
327 1st St. North
Jacksonville Beach, FL
32250

Larry Tee

"I just remember the high-pitched squeal of what seemed to be a very young, female and gay crowd. It shocked us. It seemed like the club had totally hyped us up. It was like we were The Beatles. Such energy. Looking back though, we were pretty outrageous and were quite mad ourselves. Queer and drag and unabashedly in your face."
— *Larry Tee*, Now Explosion

THEY MIGHT BE GIANTS

No. 18

Thursday, june 23
EINSTEIN▲GOGO

"I don't know why I'm remembering this but we played facing a 10,000 Maniacs poster and they brought us a seafood platter backstage. I can't remember what I ate for breakfast yesterday, but the old memories are burned in. We definitely had an Einstein A Go-Go sticker on the bottom of one of our road cases."

— JOHN LINNELL, *They Might Be Giants*

THEY MIGHT BE GIANTS

THURS.
JUNE 23

10 pm
-$7-

EINSTEIN A GO-GO
327 N. 1st ST. Jax bch   249-4646

John Flansburgh and John Linnell, 1988

Todd Beals, Sterling Bailey and King Eddie

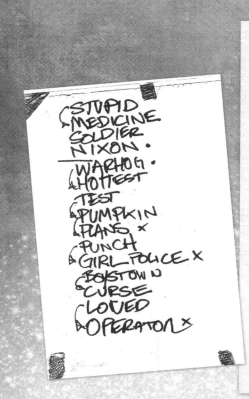

STUPID
MEDICINE
SOLDIER
NIXON •
WARHOG •
HOTTEST
TEST
PUMPKIN
PLANS ×
PUNCH
GIRL POLICE ×
BOYSTOWN
CURSE
LOVED
OPERATON ×

"One of my best
memories of
Einstein's was
dancing with my
girlfriend and
Michael Cudahy
of the band
Christmas to a
De La Soul song."

— *Walter
Rollenhagen*

JONATHAN RICHMAN

Jonathan Richman gave us his bottle of water 2.1.91 after playing at the Go-Go. He played through our amplifier & Liz & I gave him a ride to the ~~airport~~ bus station

"In 1990, Terri asked if we (Beggar Weeds) could bring one of our Fender amps out for Jonathan Richman. He was travelling by Greyhound and walked the 18 miles to the club, carrying his guitar. As Liz Hyman and I drove him back downtown after the show he grilled us about why we hadn't danced more during his performance. 'I prefer the audiences in Africa,' he said. 'They really feel it.'"

— *Scott Leuthold, Beggar Weeds*

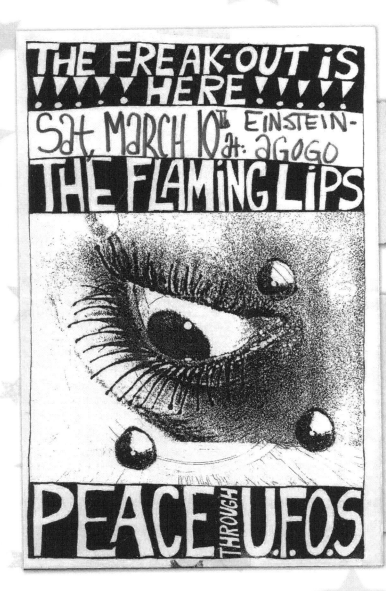

THE FREAK-OUT iS !!!!! HERE !!!!!!!
Sat. MARCH 10th at. EINSTEIN-aGoGo
THE FLAMING LIPS

PEACE THROUGH U.F.O.S

"There were only 30 people there, if I'm remembering it right, and the band was in all-black. It was super heavy, dark music with the lights down and a fog machine. That was a great show."
— *Tony Rojas*

"The Flaming Lips created a lot of noise for three guys at that time. It was lots of pedals way before everyone else was using them and lots of feedback. They were nice guys, just like dudes from Oklahoma. One thing that was awesome about Einstein A Go-Go was that you were not only meeting local and regional bands, but meeting and seeing bands from all over the world. Here was an Oklahoma band that was not even in our vocabulary at the time, and we were seeing them in this amazing little club."
— RON BURMAN

Gene Ween and Dean Ween, 1993

WEEN inConcert
FRIDAY APR .16 $ 8.00 EINSTEIN A GO - GO

EINSTEIN A GO - GO
PRESENTS:

ROBYN HITCHCOCK

pip TICKETS

IN CONCERT
SUNDAY, MAY 6TH
9:30pm $10.00

No : 84

"I remember I was so excited about that Robyn Hitchcock concert. Nirvana who?"

— *Doug Newton*

☥

"It was the night after David Bowie played in Jax and Robyn made jokes about comparing their fame and glory. It was a great show."

— *Jodi Crews*

"I was in the second 'row' behind a lovely young woman who was in rapt attention of Robyn. We were pretty much standing face to face with him." —Greg O'Rear

P.S. GREG ALSO SNAGGED AN AUTOGRAPH!

May

SUNDAY, 6...

THE ONE! TICKETS ON SALE NOW

ROBYN HITCHCOCK

Friday, 11... the fluid

ON SUB POP RECORDS

Robyn Hitchcock,1990

Einstein A GO GO
PRESENTS
Jane's Addiction
Tuesday, Feb. 7th
$12.50

No. 87

TUESDAY FEBRUARY 7

Dave Navarro, Perry Farrell and Eric Avery, 1989

JANE'S ADDICTION

"I thought there was going to be a mosh pit and the club was going to get torn up. I also thought there would be a huge fight, but it didn't happen. While it was an active crowd, it wasn't anything like we were expecting. Jane's Addiction were the most interesting people and became one of my favorite bands."

— Terri Faircloth

Missy Ponder onstage with Perry Farrell

"Einstein's created an intimate space where we felt we were not only a part of the music, but actually inside of it, like our second home. That night, Perry Farrell was there inside of our living room, blowing our minds with a show that was electric, hot, intense, sweaty, and epic. Bodysurfing, I was thrown on stage to grind it out with Perry for a song under the bright stage lights for what would be one of the most memorable moments of my Einstein's residency."

— MISSY PONDER

Hugo Largo

"When I first listened to Hugo Largo, they were definitely different from most bands. Their less-is-more approach allowed the vocals and violins to really shine while the two bassists (and no drums!) anchored their songs with a melodic percussion. You really feel like you're in a dream state listening to singer Mimi Goese's voice along with the soaring electric violin.

When Mimi sang "Second Skin" at Einstein's, she took a large chef's knife and grazed it along her neck, face and arms. She then appeared to stab herself in the gut. We were mesmerized but still filled with apprehension as it put everyone on edge. Later in the set, they provided some comic relief with a wild rendition of Bon Jovi's "Wanted Dead or Alive" that transformed the popular cheesy rock song into their style. It showed that they didn't take themselves too seriously. In fact, Mimi said that out of all the songs they played live, everyone seemed to cheer loudest for that song."

— *Marianna Whang*

Mimi Goese

Adam Peacock and Mimi Goese

142

Hugo Largo
Saturday, January 30
$5   All Ages
Einstein-A-Go Go
327 N. 1st St. Jax Beach
246-4073

Hahn Rowe

Tim Sommer

"So you had this regular touring circuit and there was a sense that there weren't any gigs down south. Then suddenly, we were invited to Jacksonville, and there was this incredibly warm, knowledgable reception right by the beach. A very rich and beautiful knife cut through our ignorance and preconceptions.

It helped me realize that not only everywhere in America, but everywhere in the world, there's a group of beautiful and strange children who want us to be supportive of alternative culture and alternative music. You depended on running into these places where you would find that beautiful 1980s college rock family, and Einstein's was part of our family."

— TIM SOMMER, *Hugo Largo*

Susan Ottaviano

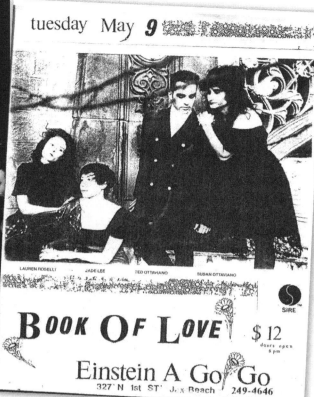

tuesday May **9**

LAUREN ROSELLI   JADE LEE   TED OTTAVIANO   SUSAN OTTAVIANO

BOOK OF LOVE $12
doors open
8 pm

Einstein A Go Go
327 N 1st ST   J.x Beach   249-4646

SIRE

"We loved Einstein's and I talked about it when we played Jacksonville again in 2019. It was one of the last of the old school punk clubs that we got to play at because very few were still around by the late '80s. What we found so endearing was that it was such a family affair. If I am correct, the daughters booked the talent and I remember the mom cooked us dinner! We had been driving for a long time and it was such a welcoming environment. I think our dressing room was the dad's workshop cluttered with tools and a table saw. I just remember it was the real deal."

— *Susan Ottaviano,* BOOK OF LOVE

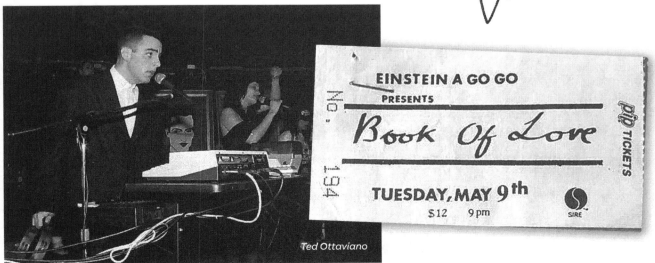

Ted Ottaviano

EINSTEIN A GO GO
PRESENTS

Book Of Love

pip TICKETS

No. 194

TUESDAY, MAY 9th
$12   9 pm

SIRE

# Poi Dog Pondering

"From 1987 to 1992, Poi Dog Pondering was calling Austin, Texas, home base and all our touring was routed out of there. We had an Econoline van with the passenger seats taken out and mattresses in their stead on the floor where we slept overnight like sardines between cities. We would drive out of Austin and head east to Baton Rouge, New Orleans, then (before heading north into Athens and the Carolinas), drive straight through Tallahassee and on to Jacksonville, Florida, where Einstein A Go-Go shimmered on the horizon.

There was only a fistful of truly wonderful workhorse touring clubs in those days that every up-and-coming band wanted to play: The Blue Note in Columbia, Missouri, Mississippi Nights in St. Louis, The Metro in Chicago, The I-Beam in San Francisco, Tipitina's in NOLA, The 40 Watt in Athens, The 9:30 Club in DC, and Einstein A Go-Go in Jacksonville.

What made Einstein's stick out was that it had a real handmade, homemade, family-fun vibe to it. They treated you like family. It was colorful and super fun to play and truly an oasis on the road. I always looked forward to it on our tour map."

— FRANK ORRALL, *Poi Dog Pondering*

"I remember everybody square dancing to the song 'Living With the Dreaming Body.' Hooking arms, dancing together in circles. I might never have remembered the song if we hadn't had so much fun dancing to it."

— *Stacy McGilvra*

FRIDAY, JANUARY **20**

"Went to see Robyn Hitchcock & the Egyptians with Poi Dog Pondering at UGA. Turned around during Poi Dog and the whole staff of Einstein's was right behind me!"

— Walter Rollenhagen

POETRY READINGS: JANUARY 25, FEBRUARY 8, 22 on WEDNESDAYs

EINSTEIN A GO-GO
327 N 1st ST., JAX BCH   ph 249 4646

ROYAL CRESCENT MOB

Harold "Happy" Chichester

David Ellison

Brian Emch

Carlton Smith

"It was one of my favorite places to play ever. I loved that it was a family operation. Bill would be there in the back where we had a makeshift dressing room and he would be frying chicken. And the all ages and younger audiences seem to have this unguarded enthusiasm."

— HAROLD "HAPPY" CHICHESTER, *Royal Crescent Mob*

Einstein a Go-Go

146

DINOSAUR JR AND SPECIAL GUEST: Rein Sanctr

SUNDAY feb 26

EINSTEIN A GO-

327 N 1st ST., JAX BCH ph 249 4646

"No club treated us as well as Einstein's. Nowhere in the country. They had a home-cooked meal for us or let us do take-out from wherever we wanted. It was like you were family."

— Lou Barlow,
Dinosaur Jr. / Sebadoh
(as told to Daniel Gill)

J. Mascis, 1989

Dinosaur jr.
WITH SPECIAL GUEST: Rein Sanction

SUNDAY, FEB 26 $8 TICKETS ON SALE NOW!

EINSTEIN A GO-GO
327 N. 1st. JAX. BCH, FL. 32250
249-4646

LIVING COLOUR
WITH GUEST: UNDERDOG

FRIDAY JUNE 17
EINSTEIN A GO-GO
327 N. 1st ST. Jax bch   249-4646

"We were sitting in front of Einstein's having one of our many band meetings and asking ourselves 'Why the hell are we doing this in the first place?' We're leaning on somebody's pickup truck and this guy comes out of the bar across the street — trucker hat, the whole nine. He goes 'Let me guess, y'all in a band? Well, that's my truck.' He assumed we were hovering around his truck waiting to do something nefarious to it when we were just having a conversation. That's what the song "Funny Vibe" is all about. We're not here to hurt anyone or do anything wrong. We're just here to play music. We're here to express ourselves. That was a major point for us in our journey and it happened in front of Einstein A Go-Go."

— COREY GLOVER, *Living Colour*

148

Muzz Skillings, Vernon Reid, Will Calhoun and Corey Glover

"I remember being in the very front for the first Living Colour show, and during the first song, lead singer Corey Glover swung his dreads and they knocked the glasses off my face."

— *Jim Leatherman*

"I went to the Living Colour show at Einstein's after work. For some reason I decided to watch the show up front by the side of the stage. I was dancing, as I often did, when Corey brought me up on stage, which freaked me out entirely (I don't like to be on stage). Honestly, I was shocked he picked me, and was flattered. That show was amazing — a very talented group of guys! I remember everyone loving that show and their positive energy."

— STEPHANIE TOTTY

Living Colour,1988

"Tammie and Terri asked me to stand at the stage when Nirvana was playing, because there weren't enough people. There were maybe 40 people there that night. Six months later, they took over the world."

— *Jonathyne Briggs*

Saturday, MAY 5th... NIRVANA

Chad Channing (drums), Krist Novoselic and Kurt Cobain, 1990

"There were more than nine people at the Nirvana show, but it was not sold out. My friend and I chatted with the bassist for a bit before the show. Kurt walked up and stood there while we were talking, but did not say anything. Kurt kept blowing fuses on his Marshall head so the set kept getting interrupted. I bought *Bleach* on CD at the Theory Shop that night."

— JAY DECOSTA PEELE

Saturday, 5 ... NIRVANA

ON SUB POP RECORDS

BULGING EYE BOOKING & MGT.
818 Brannan Ste. 202
San Francisco, CA 94103
PH:415-863-8245 FAX:415-863-9450

This contract for personal services of herein stated ARTIST on the engagement described below is made this **13th** day of **April**, 1990 between the undersigned purchaser of music(herein called PURCHASER) and stated artist in clause 1(herein called ARTIST).

1. ARTIST: Nirvana   /# of performers: 3

2. NAME/ADDRESS/PHONE # of place of engagement: Einstein a Go Go / 327 N. 1st Jacksonville Beach/ FL / 32250

3. Date of engagement: Saturday May 5 1990

4. Compensation agreed upon: $500 + 60% over $950
   Capacity: 250   Gross Potential(of room): $1250   ticket price: $5

   DEPOSIT REQUIRED: N/A   DUE DATE OF CONTRACT AND SPECIFIED DEP: April 24 1990
   (All deposits must be made payable to BULGING EYE (fed tax i.d.#00-0000000) and be in the form of a CASHIER'S CHECK or MONEY ORDER)

5. ONE PERFORMANCE of   60   minutes ONLY.

6. Payment shall be made to   Chris Novoselic   on date of engagement within 30 minutes of headliner's set.

7. Load In: 5:30
   Sound Check: 6:00
   Door Open: 8:00
   Set Time: 11:00

8. Opening/Headlining band(s):

9. Directions to the venue(please fill in) from:

10. ARTIST will have free(100%) use of PA and LIGHTING equipment.

11. ARTIST may install their own operator(s) for PA and LIGHTING if so desired. However, PURCHASER must furnish house sound man.

12. PA shall be provided by PURCHASER, at no fee to the ARTIST, and shall consist of the minimum requirements specified by rider(see attached rider).

13. LIGHTING shall be provided by PURCHASER and shall be sufficient to light stage area.

14. Stage dimensions:

15. PURCHASER agrees to provide dressing room with easy access to stage.

16. BILLING:
    (In all forms of advertising)

17. PURCHASER agrees to provide dressing room with easy access to stage.

18. PURCHASER agrees to allow no restrictions to be placed on ARTIST with regard to the sound system.

EINSTEIN A GO-GO
327 NORTH 1st STREET · JACKSONVILLE BEACH, FLORIDA

SOUL ASYLUM

tuesday, JUNE 14.

Dave Pirner and Dan Murphy

★★★★★★ *soul asylum*
EINSTEIN A GO GO
327 N.1st ST, JAX BCH
★★★★★★★★★★★★★★★★★★★★★★★★★★★★★★★★★★★★★★★

Dave Pirner

THIS IS A DOUBLE BILL
THAT SHOULD FRIGHTEN YOU.
DO YOU GET IT? FEAR.
LONG-HAIRED, TATTOED,
UNBRIDLED, PURE, LOUD,
VISCERAL FEAR....
WHICH YOU HAVE
NEVER KNOWN!~

FROM MINNEAPOLIS
ON A&M RECORDS

SOUL ASYLUM

with special guest SNATCHES OF PINK FROM N

June 14 $8

EINSTEIN A GO-GO

Grant Young

Karl Mueller

MUDDIED MEMORIES

Jason Ferguson's recollection of Mudhoney at Einstein's was central to his 2008 interview with the Seattle band for *Orlando Weekly*

MAYBE YOU WENT WITH SOME OTHER band," laughs Mark Arm. The singer and guitarist for legendary Seattle band Mudhoney is in the process of poking a giant hole in the middle of one of my favorite anecdotes. The story has a young me, circa 1990, heading off with the Mudhoney boys after a show in Jacksonville Beach. We'd been drinking all night, and after they finished playing a show at the (dearly departed) Einstein A Go-Go, we all headed down the street and happened upon a midget bar. Three-quarter-scale pool tables and all. Except the short people in this bar weren't cute, reality-TV midgets. This was a midget biker bar, with the patrons decked out in leather and bearing no patience for the intrusion of full-sized gawkers. After some threatening glances from the regulars, we decided the place wasn't for us.

I've told this tale dozens of times, once in these very pages, because the memory of this occurrence is as vivid in my mind as the day I married my wife — and now, thanks to Mark Arm, I'm digging around in my mental safe-deposit box for my marriage certificate.

"I don't remember the midget bar, but you know, if you drink enough, things can start to look a lot smaller," consoles Arm. Then, laughing, he says, "Or maybe you just did some dust."

Probably not. I'm forced to console myself with the supposition that Arm's memories of that long-ago tour stop may be a little fuzzy. After all, the guy and his band have played hundreds of shows in their 20-year existence. Maybe he just forgot this Florida midget bar?

"No, I doubt it. I'm pretty sure I'd remember a midget bar."

— *Jason Ferguson*

NOTE: Using the term "midget bar" was rude in 1990, unacceptable in 2008, and completely shameful in 2024. I'm embarrassed to have used it, but this is the story as it was told, and I apologize for it.

> "I went swimming in the ocean with Mudhoney and we were all tripping our brains out. It was the coolest thing ever."
>
> — *Tony Rojas*

> "I saw Meat Puppets play with Mudhoney. It was amazing to watch Curt Kirkwood play guitar like he was born with it in his hands."
>
> — *Bill Perry*

Saturday, Oct. 21ST... SCREAMING TREES — FROM SEATTLE ON SST RECOR... WAY COOL $5⁰⁰

friday, Oct. 28TH... BULLET LAVOLTA — LOUD ROCKERS FROM BOSTON ON TAANG REC $5⁰⁰ AT THE ...

friday, Nov. 3RD... Mudhoney & THE FLUID — HAIR INVASIO SEATTLE TWO-S NEED WE SAY MOR... $7 TICKE...

ALSO CHECK OUT IN November: MEAT PUPPETS, WINTER HOURS, TEXAS INSTRUMENTS.....

einstein a go-go — SERVING THE PUBLIC SINCE 1985 ROCKNROLL! — 327 North 1ST Street, lovely JACKSONVILLE. PHONE US AT 249-4646 (MACHINE) or 246-4...

"In the '80s, there were probably only 50,000 people in the United States who listened to college radio stations and bought that music — that was the underground rock scene until the '90s. It wasn't very many people and it was all due to college rock. That's where all the independent labels like SST and Sub Pop would sell their music. If it hadn't been for college rock, none of the '90s thing would have happened because that's where all the musicians grew up and became bands."

— Gary Lee Conner, SCREAMING TREES

"I had grown out my hair during my first year of college, and for whatever reason, it became a point of contention with my mom. I kept on denying her requests to get it cut because I had Hair Fest '91 on my calendar and wanted to be able to fully embrace the moment. The show was incredible between Screaming Trees' killer set, Das Damen's thumping cacophony and King Missile's zaniness. And the next day I was at the barber shop getting my hair snipped just in time for Mom's birthday."

— *Jon Glass*

Das Damen's Jim Walters and Alex Totino during Hair Fest '91

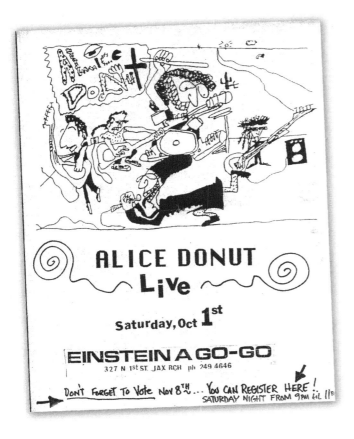

ALICE DONUT
LiVE

Saturday, Oct 1st

EINSTEIN A GO-GO
327 N 1st ST. JAX BCH ph 249 4646

Don't forget to vote Nov 8th ... You can register here!
SATURDAY NIGHT FROM 9PM til 11th

"After I moved to Tallahassee, one of the bands I booked for FSU at the Club Downunder was Alice Donut. Their singer (Tomas Antona) was a maniac. He wore this trench coat covered in psychedelic paint because he was a painter, too. In Tallahassee, he climbed up and was hanging off the side of the balcony railing with no underwear on underneath. It was one of those moments that led us to becoming friends, and I saw them again at Einstein's. When I moved to New York, I didn't know anyone other than the guys from Alice Donut. I had a day job at a booking agency for reggae, blues and R&B acts — nothing to do with the kind of music I listened to. Alice Donut really wanted me as their manager, and I ended up managing them for seven years until they broke up."

— RON BURMAN

WINDOW OF OPPORTUNITY

I BELIEVE THE YEAR WAS 1991 AND my friend Donald K. and I weren't able to get tix to the show, so we did what dimwitted 20 year olds at that point in time would do in order to see Primus for the first time — come up with a risky plan. We would scale the back wall of the metal venue that butted up to the back of EAGG which would then get us to the roof of EAGG. We knew the green room on the roof of EAGG had no glass in a window, and there were just widely spaced 2x4s that we could easily squeeze between. We thought if we timed it right Tad would still be on stage and Primus would be upstairs waiting to go on. Armed with a spliff that we planned to blaze just as we emerged through the window, we hoped it would lessen the shock of two idiots barging in on the band. We arrived and smoothly took our hiding positions between the bushes and the metal club's outdoor wooden deck (metalheads banging abound) to wait for our moment to scale the wall undetected by climbing a pipe (I can't remember if it was electrical or plumbing) that ran up the side of it. Waiting for a clean shot was taking a little longer than we thought it would. All of a sudden the back door of EAGG that opened to the little alley swung open and Primus and one unknown fellow spark up. Squatting there in the bushes we just watched and laughed quietly to ourselves. They quickly puffed, passed and went back inside. That's when we made our move up the wall and over to the green room window. When we get there no one is in the room and we immediately hear Primus launch into "To Defy." We jetted down the stairs and found Tad at the bottom by himself in what I remember being a La-Z-Boy-style chair. We thought he was dead or dying. He looked so wiped out. We offered him the J and left it with him, then slipped unnoticed into the crowd. The show was like every show at Einstein's, beautiful. I peeled a setlist off the stage after the show and ended up sitting at the bar with Tim "Herb" Alexander and Les Claypool for 15 minutes or so. We talked about fishing.

Thanks to everyone at EAGG for everything they did for all of us kids over those years. I apologize for my behavior that night and the counterfeit ticket used at the Jane's Addiction show.

— MICHAEL WHITTIER

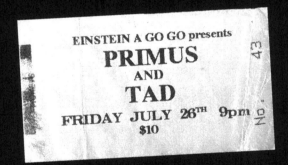

EINSTEIN A GO GO presents
PRIMUS
AND
TAD
FRIDAY JULY 26TH 9pm
$10

Tad, 1991

Les Claypool of Primus, 1991

john and mary

(that's mary ramsey of 10,000 Maniacs)

(that's john lombardo of 10,000 Maniacs)

juliana hatfield   feb. 1 $6

einstein a go-go   8pm

> "I remember meeting Juliana Hatfield after the show and her being so nice. My friend and I asked if I could take a picture with her, and I landed on her ankle as we sat on the stage for the picture. I could tell it hurt and I felt so bad. But she was polite about it."
>
> — *Amanda Smith Hiers*

THE THEORY SHOP PRESENTS;

Buffalo Tom

with *special guest:* **st johnny**

FRIDAY, FEBRUARY 11 9PM $7.50

=== **EINSTEIN A GO-GO** ===

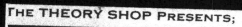

Buffalo Tom: Bill Janovitz, Chris Colbourn and Tom Maginnis (drums, not pictured), 1994

St. Johnny: Tom Leonard, Bill Whitten, Jim Elliott and Wayne Letitia (drums, not pictured), 1994

> "My friend and I tried to convince Buffalo Tom to play this really rare B-side called 'Witches' but the band did not oblige."
>
> — *Zak Champagne*

The Aquanettas: Jill Richmond, Claudine Troise, Stephanie Seymour and Deborah Schwartz

LOVE WITH
DIPLOMAT
WISHING WELL
FAULTS
PATHWAY
UNCLE SYDNEY
DISCO
CINEMATIC ANGEL
HIPPY
SEX GLAM
MIND FULL
BEACH PARTY
15 MEN
FOOTSTEPS

NEW SONG

NINE INCH TALES

WE GOT EXCELLENT FOOD AT THE VENUE, and we remember this because we usually got pretty shitty food (if anything at all) from the places we played on that tour. Debby specifically remembers receiving a fine vegetarian meal that night. The place had a really cool hipster indie feel to it. It was a bit of an oasis or an indie haven in the middle of ... well ... the rest of Florida. Corey Glover of Living Colour came to see us play and he was very nice. We were so excited that he saw our show and everyone else was pretty stoked that he was there, too. Jill and Debby visited the beach that night after the show and we ran into Nine Inch Nails at our motel. We had played with them beforehand in Texas (twice!), and when we pulled into our motel they were in the parking lot. The motel was an absolute shithole. Claudine clearly remembers bugs on the wall, stained sheets and what she believes was a stab hole from a knife in her pillow. Ah, the joys of touring!

— *Stephanie Seymour, THE AQUANETTAS*

ANYTHING COULD HAPPEN HERE

THE FIRST TIME I WENT TO EINSTEIN A GO-GO was in the summer of 1994, I was 13 years old. By the time fall hit I was going as many times a week as I could afford to with the little money I got busing tables at a pizzeria at the beach called Roberto's. I was turned on to a lot of music that year, a whole world of music that was not on the radio or MTV — underground music. My friend kept talking about a band called Sebadoh and one night he played songs from their new album *Bakesale* over the phone for me that sounded cool. That week I bought the album on cassette and would listen to it all the time. One night I got really excited when I heard Sebadoh was coming to Einstein's to play a concert. As soon as I had the money I went to the Theory Shop and got my ticket for the show.

On the night of the show my friend and I congregated at the stage pretty early. We were small dudes, so if we didn't get a good spot up front we wouldn't be able to see the band. I was basically sitting on the front of the stage where Lou Barlow was going to be singing. Once the band took the stage I was hyper attentive. They seemed so chill up there, talking, making jokes I didn't understand and playing these songs that I loved. They seemed so cool but also they just seemed like regular dudes. There was no divine rock

The Theory Shop Presents:

seBADoh

With special guest: Harry Pussy

Monday, Feb 6 1994 9p.m.
$8.50 advance $10.50 day of the show
EINSTEIN A GO-GO 327 N 1st St. Jacksonville Bch

star quality to them, no untouchable pedestal like I'd see on MTV, and they were literally a few feet away from me. This was the first time I ever thought that maybe I could be in a band and putting out cool records didn't seem like a crazy unattainable goal. Looking back I realize that night changed everything for me.

I was glued to the show, taking it all in. At one point Lou Barlow struck up the song "The Freed Pig" and I got super excited. The band made it through the first chorus and Lou broke a string and decided not to finish the song. I was bummed but also surprised. This was a far stretch from the well-choreographed shows I'd seen on TV or at big stadium concerts. It seemed like anything could happen here. Toward the end of the show, the drummer lost control of one of his sticks midsong. It went flying and hit me in the head. Without skipping a beat he grabbed another stick and kept playing. I could see him mouthing a sincere apology to me from behind the drums, but I just smiled and waved like "It's cool." I went home that night with new eyes, a loud ringing in my ears and a drumstick from my favorite band. Gimme Indie Rock!

— RICK COLADO
(a.k.a rickoLus)

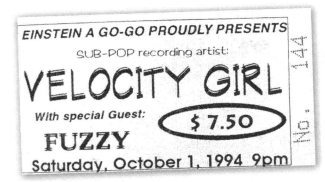

EINSTEIN A GO-GO PROUDLY PRESENTS

SUB-POP recording artist:

VELOCITY GIRL

With special Guest: **$ 7.50**

FUZZY

Saturday, October 1, 1994 9pm

Kelly Young and Sarah Shannon

Zachary Boyle with Sarah Shannon

Jim Spellman (drums) and Brian Nelson

"Velocity Girl was one of my favorite bands. I saw the video for "Crazy Town" on *120 Minutes* and was slightly obsessed — like a typical 15 year old might be now with Taylor Swift. After the show I was lucky enough to meet Sarah Shannon and take a photo. I remember being shocked she was smoking. With a voice like hers I didn't think she should smoke (naive teenage dreams crushed). I also met Archie Moore who was wearing an Unrest T-shirt, which I liked. He and Sarah were polite, but preoccupied. I didn't take it personally though. The rest of the band could not have been nicer, especially Kelly Young and Brian Nelson. They kindly chatted about music and posed for photos. The access to the bands, and the willingness and expectation to interact with us kids was one of the many things that made Einstein's so special."

— *Zachary Boyle*

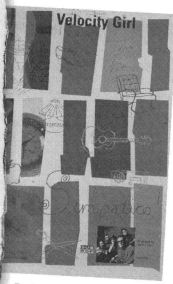

Zachary's autographed poster

Hilken Mancini and David Ryan (drums) of Fuzzy

the cranberries

IN CONCERT **tuesday**
showtime **july**
at 9:30 **6**

tickets on sale at
the **THEORY SHOPS**
$8.50

ON ISLAND RECORDS

EINSTEIN A GO·GO
327 N 1st ST Jacksonville Beach ph 249-4646 for info

"I was first in line and up front for the show. Dolores came out with really short hair and wearing Doc Martens. She was just so powerful and connected to her music. This was during a kind of volatile time in my life when my mom had just died and I was struggling with my identity and people's expectations. Talk about girl power, I left there and felt like I could take over the universe. I promptly shaved my head — just left my bangs and shaved the rest off. 'I can be whoever I want. I can look however I want. I don't care. It's like super cool and not weird.' That will forever be a seminal moment in my life."

— WENDY CAMPBELL

166

Mike Hogan, Dolores O'Riordan,
Fergal Lawler and Noel Hogan, 1993

"We'd heard about the legendary shows
before our time like Jane's Addiction and
10,000 Maniacs so we wanted that for
ourselves. The Cranberries show was that
for us — our holy grail. A few of us got to
hang out with them on the tour bus. I still
have the red T-shirt they all signed with
Sharpies. Also, Dolores gave me a small
stuffed bear. I was on cloud nine."

— *Jenny Thomas Medure*

nberries
TUESDAY, july 6th
EINSTEIN A GO-GO
9:30PM $8.50
on island records

No. 203

"I was working in July '93 when The Cranberries were playing at the club, and I was asked to bring a tray of snacks to the band room. I went through the doorway at the side of the stage and as I was passing the bathroom the door opened and out came Dolores completely bare-breasted. My jaw dropped as I fumbled with the tray attempting to cover my eyes. She began laughing as if she'd just heard the funniest joke. 'American,' she declared."

— *Bruce Tomecko*

JAX KIDS KNEW

I WAS IN A LONGWOOD, FLORIDA, CLUB CALLED Fern Park Station when I saw another band setting up while we were waiting for The Posies. Unbelievably, I heard someone say it was "some band called The Cranberries." I went "holy shit!" I'd only brought two rolls of film so I ran to Eckerd and bought 10 more. When I got back everyone was in the back drinking beer and not paying attention to The Cranberries at all so it felt like my own private show. I was singing along with the songs and taking pictures. At the end of the show, the minute they were done, Dolores came up to me and said, "How do you know all the words?" I told her I worked at a record store, had an advance copy of their first album for three months and that I loved them. She said, "I can tell." We struck up a longer conversation at the bar with all four of the band members just drinking and talking about life. As we were calling it a night, they said, "we're playing in Jacksonville tomorrow at Einstein A Go-Go." So I took off work early and drove to Jacksonville. Tammie let me in early so I got to watch the soundcheck and asked if I could take pictures of them on the beach. We also ended up shopping in the Theory Shop and Dolores bought the Metallica/Guns N' Roses shirt she wore that night on stage. Getting to see The Cranberries at their earliest point in America and to see them become the band that they became, you can't beat that. We got to see them in a little bitty club with a really good crowd, too, as far as the number of people who came out that night. The kids in Jacksonville knew who they were whereas the people in Orlando didn't know who they were at all.

— *Jim Leatherman*

IN CONCERT

MADDER ROS

Monday, June 2
EINSTEIN A GO-GO
9:30pm 327 N. 1st Street Jacksonville Beach

The Theory Shop Presents;
IN CONCERT

MERCURY REV

Sunday, November 5 1995 9 PM
$7.50
Einstein A Go-Go 327 N 1st St Jax Bch

No. 224

A MUSIC SHOP PRODUCTION

FLESHTONE

saturday 28
FEBRUARY
EINSTEIN A GO-GO
327 N 1st St. JAX BCH.

No. 68

The THEORY SHOP Presents;
in concert

{unrest}

WITH SPECIAL GUEST:
SLANT 6
WEDNESDAY, FEBRUARY 9
SHOW STARTS AT 9PM
EINSTEIN A GO-GO 👉 $5.50

No. 96

SATURDAY JUNE 11

SUGARSMACK

WITH SPECIAL GUEST TRINKET
Einstein A Go-Go

THE MUSIC SHOP PRESENTS:

NEW MODEL ARMY

SUNDAY, AUGUST 2 SEVEN
EINSTEIN A GO
327 N 1st ST JAX BCH

No. 76

THE MUSIC SHOP PRESENTS:

LONG RYDERS

WITH SPECIAL GUEST: beggar weeds
SUNDAY, july 12 9 PM
EINSTEIN A GO GO $8

pip TICKETS

fIREHOSE

AND
SCREAMING TREES

SUNDAY, APRIL 17 9pm E.A.G.G.

No. 65

pip TICKETS
6.00 advan
A MUSIC SHOP PRODUCTIO

THE DEAD MILK
Thursday oct. 1

CONCERT

LORELEI

FRIDAY, APRIL $6.00
at
EINSTEIN A GO GO
327 N 1ST ST Jacksonville BEACH
APRIL 5 1996 STAR

EINSTEIN A GO-GO PRESENTS

MARY'S DANISH

Sunday, Feb. 3rd.
9:30 P.M. $8.00

No. 32

EINSTEIN A G
249 · GO GO (464
* no refunds

No. 23

EINSTEIN A GO GO PRESENTS

DREAMS SO REAL

$8 **FRIDAY, JUNE 16**

No. 18

THE MUSIC SHOP PRESENTS:

GREEN ON RED

ON MERCURY RECORDS
SATURDAY, MAY 10 doors open at 8 PM
EINSTEIN A GO-GO
327 N. 1ST ST. JAX BCH (PH.) 246-4073

IN CONCERT

Swirlie

THURSDAY APRIL
9PM $4.50
EINSTEIN A GO-

The Theory Shop Presents;
IN CONCERT

Luna

Friday Jan 26, 1996
$7.50
EINSTEIN A GO-GO 327 N 1st St Ja

EINSTEIN A GO-GO PRESENTS

sloan and special g
HAMMERB

8 PM JUNE 6 SUNDAY $8.0

EINSTEIN A GO-GO pre

drivin' n'cry

with special guest; Rein Sa
Friday, August 12

THE BUCK PETS
Sunday, March 3rd
10 pm $6

EINSTEIN A GO-GO
327 N 1st ST. JAX BCH (246-4073)
PRESENTS:
ELEKTRA RECORDING ARTIST:
10,000 MANIACS
SATURDAY MARCH 22
Doors open at 8PM $5

EINSTEIN A GO GO
PRESENTS
Dumptruck
Saturday, Oct 8th

No. 380

pic recording artist:
Living Colour
aturday, Oct 29 10pm $7

AM RECORDING ARTIS
SWIMMING POOL Q's
SATURDAY · JULY 5 · 10PM
EINSTEIN A GO-GO · 329 N 1st ST. JAX BCH

SST Recording ARTIST:
Dinosaur jr
WITH SPECIAL GUEST:
REIN SANCTION
Sunday. Feb 26th
AT
Einstein A GO-GO 327 N 1st ST. JAX
pip TICKETS
SHOWS AT 9PM
EIGHT DOLLARS

UNREST TH FAITH HEALERS
SUPERCHUNK
$8.00
EINSTEIN A GO-GO FEB. 26
NO S

EINSTEIN A GO-GO
PRESENTS
LOVE TRACTOR
FRIDAY, Oct 7TH
Are you
pip TICKETS
No.
11

EINSTEIN A GO GO PRESENT
VIOLENT FEMMES
with special guest
HICKASAW MUDD PUPPIES
urday, march 31 9
$15

EINS IN A GO-GO PRESENTS:
ROYAL CRESCENT MOB
SATURDAY, DEC 10

EINSTEIN A GO GO PRESENTS.
MONDAY, MARCH 28
Meat Puppets
& BEGGAR WEEDS
No. 456

Einstein A Go - Go Presents
KILLING JOKE
aturday, August 5 $7.00

Elektra RECORDING ARTIST:
X
sunday, nov 1 10pm

EINSTEIN a GO

Einstein a GO-GO
PRESENTS
SWANS
Thursday, Sept. 21   10 pm
$7.00

IN CONCERT
CROWSDEL
Poster Childr
9 PM $6.00 LIVE
first

Einstein A Go - Go
Presents:
Faith No More
Friday, Dec. 8, 10:30 P.M.
$8.00

pip TICKETS

instein A GO GO
PRESENTS
e FEELIES
& YO LA TANGO
urday, Feb. 4th

RED HOT CHILI PEPPERS
wed
dec 2
No. 306
$12
pip TICKETS
FAITH NO MORE

SONIC YOUTH
With Special Guest; B.A.L.L.
riday, Dec 2CND $8

CLUB CULTURE

Stylish club kids, 1989

COME AS YOU ARE

T HE "FOUNTAIN OF SONIC YOUTH" BANNER hanging behind the bar was more than just a playful twist on Ponce de León's sought-after magical spring supposedly hidden in nearby St. Augustine. The colorful chalk-drawn sign was a testament that Einstein's itself was a destination for discovery.

Without a doubt, musical finds were uncovered nearly every night throughout the club. There were the I'll-never-ever-forget moments when your favorite band graced the Einstein's stage. Or, the downtimes you spent flipping through the Theory Shop bins in search of an obscure indie act's CD or that New Order 12-inch import to take home at the end of your night. And probably more than ever, there were the moments when the DJ dropped the needle on a track that would catapult you from the red-vinyl booths to your self-claimed spot on the dance floor. "Dancing is where your 'musical-taste chocolate' got into someone else's 'musical-taste peanut butter,'" Christopher Hooker explains. "It served to unite us."

The club's all-ages approach served as its own invitation for you to feel part of the extended Einstein's family for a night or as long as you'd like. "When I look back at it, this place was really ahead of its time in that it was inclusive whether that was race, gender or identity," recalls Mike Triplett, guitarist for Fin Fang Foom. "It was a place that everyone could go to feel comfortable no matter what they wore or who they were."

Because our attire, tastes or attitude weren't always fully understood by others, Einstein's was the safe haven from our daily lives. At some schools, the nickname "Steiner" was used to distinguish us from the jocks, rich kids, nerds and others in the stereotypical social class vernacular we used. Einstein's certainly had its cliques, however, these labels didn't really matter. Kristin Terrill Reeder no longer felt like the "weird kid" when she was at Einstein's because everyone there was a weird kid in some way. "You were finally just you, and that was a very profound thing particularly for an introverted, nervous, anxious, shy kid like myself," Kristin says.

In a place where your guard didn't always have to be up, you had the freedom to seek out whatever – or whoever – made you happy, too. "There was always a little bit of magic inside the walls of the club," Jenny Thomas Medure says. "It was a place where your heart would skip a beat, those hormones could rage a little bit and sparks would sometimes fly if you caught the eye of your crush on the other side of the dance floor."

Whatever quest you were on, you almost certainly could find it at Einstein's. That is why we cherish and miss it as much as we do today. We were fortunate enough to have a chance to splash around in that Fountain of Sonic Youth.

— *Jon Glass*

FANS CAME FROM ALL OVER

"We would drive two and a half hours from Valdosta. I remember dodging deer one night taking the back roads through Baker County."

— Walter Rollenhagen

"On the drive from **Kingsland** to see Book of Love in 1989, I had a flat tire at the Florida-Georgia line. I was totally goth to the max that night. I was kneeling beside the passenger rear tire when a car full of older people pulled up behind me to help. When I stood up and faced them they had a total look of horror and the old women were yelling at the driver to 'Just go get out of here' before they sped off. LOL. I made it to the club in time and it was a great show."

— GARY C. DANIELS

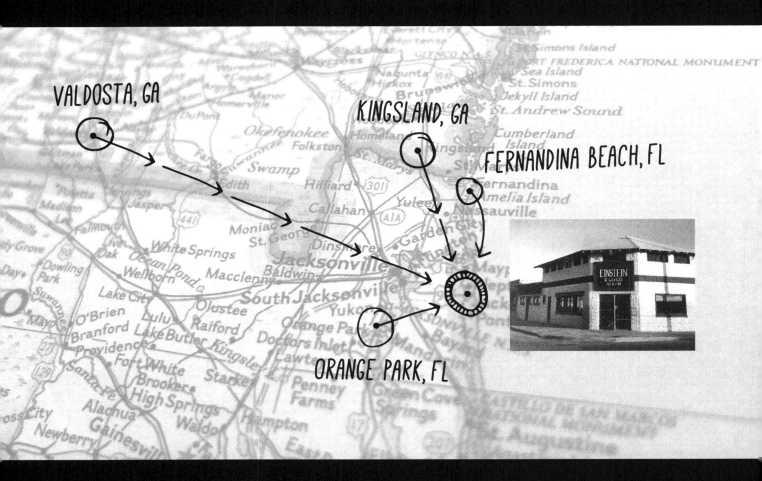

"I lived in **Orange Park**. The ride itself with friends was fun, but it was long. Combined with a midnight curfew it meant having to leave at around 11 p.m. That part was not great and I still appreciate my friends leaving earlier than they had to for me so that I could go."

— Gunnar Jurdzik

"I grew up in **Fernandina Beach**. I have fond memories of loading up my car with anyone I could, and dragging them 30-plus miles, sometimes picking up more peeps on the way, to experience something beyond our isolated little island community. I loved EAGG and we made that trip at least once a week for years."

— Richard Wade

IT'S NOT JUST FOR KIDS ANYMORE

IN 1988 I WAS A COOK IN THE NAVY stationed far from my Pennsylvania home aboard the *USS Forrestal* CVA-59. This Super Carrier Vessel was a floating city with more than 5,000 people who expected to be served chow 16 hours a day. When not out to sea, we were docked at Mayport Naval Station near Jax Beach.

Working as a cook was hot, stressful, hard physical labor that required spending long days and nights on your feet preparing and serving food with 20 other guys. We did get to have a boombox in the kitchen to ease the long hours, but with very little storage space on the huge ship, each guy had just a handful of his favorite cassettes. I was the only white guy on my shift and the music we listened to reflected the majority choice, which ran from hip-hop, rap, MC Hammer, and Tony! Toni! Toné! among others. I rarely got the chance to play the few I'd brought from home. My favorite was a mixtape full of college radio songs. I also had some Smiths, The Clash and a cool new one: They Might Be Giants. Most of the time I got a laugh out of the galley for playing my music.

One time I was playing one of my cassettes when another cook said, "Hey, that group (The Clash) is awesome." He told me to check out this club called Einstein's the next time we got into port. He said, "They play good music, but it's just a bunch of kids pogoing around and they don't serve alcohol."

When I was back in Mayport I started looking for this club by asking around, checking the phone book (no internet back then). Finally, someone said, "Oh, that's out at Jax Beach. You'll have to take Bus No. 16 to get there," because I didn't have a car back in those days.

So I went on a Thursday night when there were maybe 13 people in the club including the staff. The Church's "Reptile" was playing and kids were dancing around doing that sort of goth dance, like in a triangle. I thought it was cool, weird and fun. I was shy and a little awkward, so I ordered a "smart drink"

from the bartender and made my way to the back of the club. I started looking at the records and merchandise in the Theory Shop where Mrs. Faircloth gave me a wide smile and started telling me things about Einstein's. She introduced me to some fascinating people that night — Joe Scully, Marianna, Allison, Dancing Todd, and, of course, Terri and Tammie. They had that Southern hospitality kind of thing that made me feel welcomed.

After that, any time I was off the ship I usually spent at EAGG. I saw so many now legendary bands and met some brilliant musicians. Living Colour was the first of so many incredible shows I saw at Einstein's! One of the highlights of my life was when I saw Chris Cornell and Soundgarden hanging out at Peeler's, a nearby bar, making fun of the bad hair metal band that was playing. I also got to hang out with Jane's Addiction before their show, eat food with bands after shows, and skinny-dip with The Connells after a brutally hot night. The memories are amazing and vivid.

It was a little sad when I got out of the Navy, got a job, and moved to an apartment in Riverside; it was just too far to go out to Einstein's on a regular basis. Like so many others, I still miss my time there. It was a unique and inspirational experience. I still rock my EAGG T-shirts. I have one of the original ones framed on my wall.

Music is life! I will always remember Marianna making a poster that said "Fountain of Sonic Youth" to hang above the bar. I couldn't agree more.

— Dennis "Spyder" Donecker

Dennis Donecker was stationed on the USS Forrestal, 1996

DANCE

"Alternative became the next big deal and kids were seeing it on MTV. They're like, 'Wow, I really like this!' And then they find out there's a place to hear it in Jacksonville! It was a confluence of really great music coming out with the punk scene exploding — a perfect storm of everything and Einstein's was a part of that. It sustained a lot of kids through the bullshit of junior high and high school, and maybe even into college. At Einstein's, you didn't have to worry about it. You just danced your ass off all night."

— *Joel Totty*

Dance

"Einstein's is where I learned to just dance how I wanted to dance. I didn't care, I never needed an invitation, and I never needed anyone to ask me. And that's how I live my life. If I want to dance, I'm going to dance and I don't need an invitation."

— Denise Reagan

DANCE

Dance

"I liked the fact that you could dance at Einstein's and nobody bothered you. Everybody had their bubble of personal space and we were there just to have a good time, dance and enjoy the music."
— *Angela Turk*

"My favorite spot was pretty much a right angle from the DJ booth and the left speaker. There was always something about being close to the DJ that made it more magical."
— Michael J. Allen

The main emphasis of EINSTEIN A GO GO IS MUSIC!

"I was in high school and wasn't allowed to go to Einstein's so I had to sneak out. I remember being nervous to dance and just sitting there scared. But then my favorite song came on and I'm like, 'Alright, I'm just going to do it.' I got up and danced hoping nobody was looking at me. Once you're out there, it's fine. It's probably the best therapy to get out there, not think about anything and just dance."

— *Tracy Shedd*

"I didn't understand it at the time, but we all had some sort of deep-seated emotional problems and some of us just had high school problems. This club was therapy for a lot of kids. People could talk to Tammie and Terri then dance away their problems. Forlorn about lost love? Music is the therapy."
— *Michael Virzera, aka DJ Dr. Strangelove*

"The common thread was the music. We all loved the music. We may not have all loved all of the bands collectively, but we all loved what we loved and enjoyed a music fest every friggin' weekend."
— *Stephanie Totty*

"Tammie only wanted us to play shoegaze music at midnight or later. Matt Hopkins was a DJ at the time and he would put on some new song (let's just say it was Ride's 'Vapour Trail,') around midnight and come down onto the dance floor by himself. He would face the speakers and do this type of dancing where he was also air guitaring, but it was a very fluid thing. That became the shoegaze dance and that's just the way a lot of kids danced at Einstein's for the next couple years."
— *Chris Mondia*

FUN·FUN·FUN·FUN·
FUN·FUN·FUN·FUN·FUN
DANCE MUSIC
FROM 8PM til 12
only $2 cover
A Hodge Podge of Musical Delites Hosted by St. Jonathyne
FUN·FUN·FUN·FUN
FUN·FUN·FUN·
FUN·FUN·FUN
9 PM
Showcase
featuring
Rhino
9 PM
TUESDAY
its More
THE
DE
MI
TICKE

WHY DO YOU ALL DANCE LIKE THAT?

ONCE, WHILE ON A DATE IN JAX Beach, my mother strolled by the club on a night I wasn't there. On a whim, she decided to do a walk-through. What was this place her Black child was going to every other weekend — this Einstein's establishment that sent her honor-roll student home with cigarette smoke sunk deep in her skin?

I don't remember whether it was Terri or Tammie who warmly welcomed Mama and let her in for free, just that my friends who'd spotted her called me laughing about it the next day. I'd thought my mother was teasing when she came home and told me about her pop-in — sometimes she did find it funny to mortify teenage me, as I was so easily and often mortified back then — but I should have known the truth by the one question she asked: Why do you all dance like that?

I wish I'd known what to say in that moment other than "I don't know ... Because!" Now that I'm the same age my mother was then (actually older... yikes!), I imagine she wasn't judging me at all, simply curious. Curious to know something about me that I couldn't articulate, even to myself, about that mysterious ritual we performed in front of the wall of sound.

I still don't have a succinct explanation for her, or for you, about why I think we danced like that. Just more questions that get closer to the feeling of it.

Like: Do you remember waiting all night for a song? Writing its title on a strip of an old concert flier and slipping it into the DJ's mailbox? Sitting with your friends on the bench underneath the glass-block window, hoping your song gets played before your curfew?

Do you remember finally hearing that riff you've pined for and running out to the dance floor, and claiming your spot? Do you remember the voice in your head that screamed I LOVE THIS FUCKING SONG and the song that you fucking loved blaring so loud it pinned your ears back?

> ## Do you remember the voice in your head that screamed I LOVE THIS FUCKING SONG?

Do you remember closing your eyes because it was almost too much — the music shaking your body, the lyrics shaking your soul, your friends right beside you but giving you space, and the sense you belonged?

Because yeah, I still do.

I turn on "Vapour Trail" now and muscle memory kicks in. I flap my hands and shake my hips and roll my shoulders. I do those little kicks with my feet and I close my eyes like I did at 16 and sing to the ceiling — la la la laaaaa, la — and when the instrumental comes on, washing over me like that wave on the cover of Ride's *Nowhere*, I can feel all y'all around me, forever young and caught up too.

— *Dawnie Walton*
Author of *The Final Revival of Opal & Nev*

Dawnie Walton, 1993

Cool Your Boots Ride

Don't Let's Start (TMBG)

Unrest
Cath Carroll

Living Colour
"Broken Heart" (Live) (come on. for old times sake!)

Hole
Violet

POSTER CHILDREN
DYNAMITE CHAIR

Schizophrenia
Sonic Youth

10,000 Maniacs-
These are the
Days
—over—

Mercury
Rev
trickle
Down

Husker Du

Eight Miles High

The Spirotsan Green
CHARLATANS
UK
You Can Sleep With My Sister
If You Play It.

FOOL'S GOLD
The Stone Roses

My Bloody Valentine
You're still in a dream

Archers of Loaf
Plumb Line

Cocteau Twins
Lorelei

HEY MR. (MS.) DJ

Tammie & Jeremiah in the DJ booth

"It was very much learning how to control the room with energy. Some of the DJs would get good energy, get people pumping, and then they'd put it in slow drive. That's not gonna work. You have to let your energy build, and then you bring it back down. You build and build and build, then you bring it back, and at the end of the night you play things that people can't dance to just to introduce it. Jonathyne and Ricky were probably the best because they understood how to get the energy going. You can't think, 'What do I think is cool? What do I think they should listen to?' No, because you're there to entertain people. So what you do is you provide an energy and then they feed off that and you feed off them."

— *Tammie Faircloth*

playlist by
DJ JONATHYNE BRIGGS

Discovering the Alternative Nation. A playlist of songs from the summer of 1990 at Einstein's, likely played in the 11 o'clock hour with the smoke machine pumping and the disco ball spinning.

DEPECHE MODE "Personal Jesus"

NINE INCH NAILS "Down In It"

SINÉAD O'CONNOR "I am Stretched on Your Grave"

URBAN DANCE SQUAD "Deeper Shade of Soul"

DIGITAL UNDERGROUND "The Humpty Dance"

SOHO "Hippychick"

THE CHARLATANS "The Only One I Know"

THE SOUP DRAGONS "I'm Free"

HAPPY MONDAYS "Step On"

SONIC YOUTH "Kool Thing"

JANE'S ADDICTION "Stop!"

PIXIES "Dig for Fire"

COCTEAU TWINS "Iceblink Luck"

THE SUNDAYS "Here's Where the Story Ends"

THE TRASHCAN SINATRAS "Obscurity Knocks"

Einstein a Go Go
327 n 1st st, jax bch

We had little slips of paper that people could write their song requests on and put in the mailbox. I'd arrange playlists around the requests and figure out how to maximize it so that at 11:30 on a Friday night every person in the club was dancing. That was always the goal — to have this moment where I look up and can see no space on the floor. Eventually I developed a system where between 8 and 9 I'd introduce newer songs, then between 9 and 10 I'd play songs people were asking for. From 10 to midnight it was the songs in heavy rotation followed by some oldies or something new. At 1:30 I'd play something weird like a Revolting Cocks song so they'd know it was time to go home.

— DJ Jonathyne Briggs

playlist by
DJ RICKY HATTAWAY

FUGAZI	"Waiting Room"
DINOSAUR JR.	"Freak Scene"
SONIC YOUTH	"Drunken Butterfly"
THE CURE	"Just Like Heaven"
THE SMITHS	"This Charming Man"
SIOUXSIE & THE BANSHEES	"Peek-A-Boo"
PETER MURPHY	"Cuts You Up"
MODERN ENGLISH	"I Melt with You"
JAMES	"Laid"
THE JESUS & MARY CHAIN	"Head On"
MY BLOODY VALENTINE	"Soft as Snow"
CATHERINE WHEEL	"I Want to Touch You"
CHAPTERHOUSE	"Pearl"
THE CRANBERRIES	"Linger"
THE SUGARCUBES	"Birthday"
NEW ORDER	"Ceremony"
PET SHOP BOYS	"West End Girls"

"My DJ strategy was something Tammie Faircloth taught me. Not a lot of DJs do this but it worked well for me: Always play three-song sets — three songs that are geared to a particular audience. Then that third song and the first song of the next set need to have some sort of overlap appeal. If I played Dinosaur Jr., Sonic Youth and Pixies, then bam, there's an indie rock set. Then I could take Pixies and go into a different genre and keep the same three people dancing for those next three songs. After that I could get others to join them on the floor and the original three will stay. Tammie taught me to build an audience that way. 'If you like this song, you might like this one, or this band.' I used that method with customers in the Theory Shop, too. 'Hey, if you like this, this and this, what are three things those bands might have in common? Check out this band.' There was some sort of appeal for me at 19 years old and I still use that logic to build my career at Merrill Lynch."

— *DJ Ricky Hattaway*

"DJing was basically trying to figure out how to transition to the next song. Even though you want to play all this other stuff, you've got to find a segue into the next song." — *DJ Christian Mendez*

DJ Matt Hopkins

A MIXTAPE BY DJ MATT HOPKINS

THE STONE ROSES	"Going Down"
JAMES	"Born of Frustration"
SPIREA X	"Chlorine Dream"
PALE SAINTS	"Babymaker"
MY BLOODY VALENTINE	"Only Shallow"
CURVE	"Fait Accompli"
THE JESUS & MARY CHAIN	"Far Gone & Out"
THE CURE	"High"
CLAN OF XYMOX	"At the End of the Day"
THE SUGARCUBES	"Hit"
RIGHT SAID FRED	"I'm Too Sexy"
POSTER CHILDREN	"If You See Kay"
FISHBONE	"Sunless Saturday"
ROBYN HITCHCOCK & THE EGYPTIANS	"So You Think You're in Love"
DIF JUZ	"No Motion"
COCTEAU TWINS	"Eggs and Their Shells"
DEAD CAN DANCE	"Cantara"
SLOWDIVE	"Catch the Breeze"
KITCHENS OF DISTINCTION	"He Holds Her, He Needs Her"
LUSH	"Monochrome"
MY BLOODY VALENTINE	"Blown a Wish"
CURVE	"Frozen"
RIDE	"Leave Them All Behind"

PLAYLIST BY DJ BRUCE TOMECKO

YO LA TENGO
"Speeding Motorcycle"

VIOLENT FEMMES
"Add It Up"

PIXIES
"Monkey Gone to Heaven"

NIRVANA
"Come As You Are"

MUDHONEY
"Sweet Young Thing
Ain't Sweet No More"

SONIC YOUTH
"Dirty Boots"

BEASTIE BOYS
"Hey Ladies"

A TRIBE CALLED QUEST
"Can I Kick It"

HAPPY MONDAYS
"Step On"

THE STONE ROSES
"Fools Gold"

RIDE
"Vapour Trail"

CATHERINE WHEEL
"Black Metallic"

LUSH
"Sweetness & Light"

COCTEAU TWINS
"Lorelei"

SIOUXSIE & THE BANSHEES
"Dear Prudence"

THE CURE
"Boys Don't Cry"

THE SMITHS
"Girlfriend in a Coma"

KENDRA SMITH
"Stars Are in Your Eyes"

10,000 MANIACS
"What's the Matter Here?"

R.E.M.
"Fall On Me"

BEGGAR WEEDS
"Churchin'"

DJ Bruce Tomecko

DJ CHRIS STESEN REMEMBERS
THE NIGHT GRUNGE ARRIVED...

"You never played the same song twice in one night, but with 'Smells Like Teen Spirit,' we did. It was that good. It was literally, stop everything. We looked at each other. What? What is this? It was amazing. It was absolutely incredible. It changed the vibe of things because it was more guitar-oriented. Nobody danced to a song they didn't know. That night we did."

What a selection !

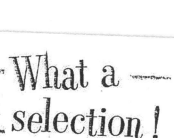

CHAPTERHOUSE "Pearl"
HAPPY MONDAYS "Kinky Afro"

THE STONE ROSES "I Am The Resurrection"
THE CHARLATANS "The Only One I Know"

MY BLOODY VALENTINE "Soon"
RIDE "Vapour Trail"

SOUNDGARDEN "Jesus Christ Pose"
THE SMASHING PUMPKINS "Siva"

THE JESUS AND MARY CHAIN
"Reverence"

THE BOO RADLEYS "Lazarus"
MINISTRY "Burning Inside"

MY LIFE WITH THE THRILL KILL KULT "Sex on Wheelz"
FRONT 242 "Headhunter"

NINE INCH NAILS "Head Like A Hole"
NIRVANA "Smells Like Teen Spirit"

PLAYLIST BY **DJ CHRIS STESEN**

EINSTEIN A GO-GO
327 N. 1st. JAX. BCH, FL. 32250
249-4646
246-4073

ea go go
BIGGER
FUCKING
SOUND

PLAYLIST BY DJ JESS BOWERS

CHAPTERHOUSE	"Pearl"
MY BLOODY VALENTINE	"Soon"
THE CHARLATANS	"The Only One I Know"
RIDE	"Vapour Trail"
KITCHENS OF DISTINCTION	"Drive That Fast"
BLUR	"There's No Other Way"
BUFFALO TOM	"Velvet Roof"
SONIC YOUTH	"My Friend Goo"
PIXIES	"Alec Eiffel"
DINOSAUR JR.	"Just Like Heaven"
SCREAMING TREES	"Nearly Lost You"
THROWING MUSES	"Not Too Soon"
ARRESTED DEVELOPMENT	"Tennessee"
DIGABLE PLANETS	"Rebirth of Slick [Cool Like Dat]"
US3	"Cantaloop [Flip Fantasia]"
POI DOG PONDERING	"U Li La Lu"
BLAKE BABIES	"Out There"
TEENAGE FANCLUB	"The Concept"
BOB MOULD	"See A Little Light"
THE CHILLS	"Heavenly Pop Hit"

"DJing for me wasn't necessarily about expressing myself. It was more of a collaboration between me and the people in the club."

— *DJ Jess Bowers*

College ~ Alternative Radio
"Dangerous Exposure" on WFYV
ROCK 105 SUNDAYS 8-10 PM

* co-produced by The Einstein A Go-Go
~ Rock 105 has a new program director... we need your cards and letters...write the station
    WFYV
    9090 Hogan Road
    Jax, FL. 32211
~ thanks! Rose, Artie, Terri, Tammie ~

Bands coming to the Einstein A Go-Go...
    Sept. 21 ~ The Swans
        22 ~ Alex Chilton w/Texas Inst.
        30 ~ Beggar Weeds

DANGEROUS EXPOSURE

In 1989 Tammie and Terri co-produced a weekly college/alternative radio show on local station Rock 105 with DJs Artie Roth and Rose Imperato.

CELEBRATIONS

EINSTEIN a GO-GO

BILL! →

"The night before my wedding, we didn't have a 'bachelor party,' I had a party at my house. We had a few people there and all piled in the car and went to Einstein's and basically took over the club. We were all dancing in a big circle and it's just a blur in my mind of just, like, the end of being single (obviously), the end of childhood, I'd just graduated from college and it was this magical bookend."

— Jess Bowers

The silence when
doors open wide
where people
could pay to see
inside
for entertainment
they watch
his body twist
behind his eyes
he says
i still exist
This is the way,
step inside.

Ian Curtis

NO EXIT volume 3

einstein a go go 327 n. 1st st. jax bch

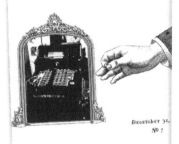

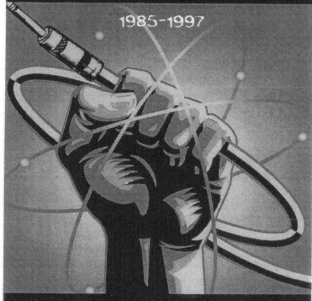

EINSTEIN A GO-GO

1985-1997

GREAT SPIRITS HAVE ALWAYS FOUND VIOLENT OPPOSITION FROM MEDIOCRITIES.
ALBERT EINSTEIN

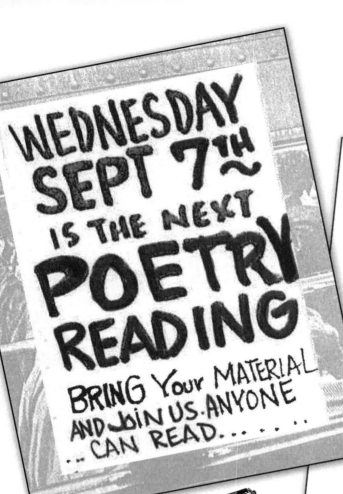

WEDNESDAY SEPT 7TH ~ IS THE NEXT POETRY READING

BRING Your MATERIAL AND JOIN US. ANYONE CAN READ........

Support Human Rights

Don't miss the

AMENSTY BENEFIT CONCERT
SATURDAY, MARCH 2
5-11 PM $6

featuring Live music by

AFTERNOON BLIND
VISHNU
THE CADETS
and more....

To be held at **EINSTEIN A GO-GO**
327 N 1st ST Jax Bch
call 249-4646 for info

Einstein A Go-Go will be open til 2AM
with dance music after the show
A portion of proceeds go to AMNESTY

Wed, june 27
a play by Wallace Stevens

Bowl, cat
and
Broomstick

two dollars

Einstein A Go-Go
327 N. 1st street
Ph# 249-4646 / 246-4073

RIGHT WHALES BENEFIT
Beggar Weeds & crosskill

SUNDAY, JULY 2

Einstein A Go-Go

LIVE MUSIC STARTS AT 8PM

FINE DOLLAR DONATION AT THE DOOR

PROCEEDS GO TO THE RESEARCH AND PRESERVATION OF THE ATLANTIC RIGHT WHALE.

ENTER THE MORRISEY VIDEO CONTEST
EVERY-ONE WINS!
JUST ASK FOR DETAILS

FREE ALBUMS POSTERS

MORRISEY RECORD RELEASE PARTY SUNDAY 6 PM til 10 PM

GROUPS, SOLO ACTS, POETS WE'RE LOOKING FOR YOU. TO JOIN US...

OPEN MIC WEDNESDAY'S EVERY WEEK FROM 8 PM til

ADMISSION $2.00
TO SIGN UP CALL IN ADVANCE 246-4073
THE MUSIC
ASK FOR TER

HELP DEVELOP LOCAL TALENT BY SUPPORTING IT!

327 N. 1st ST EINSTEIN A GO-

the Einstein A Go-Go FAMILY would like to meet your FAMILY

bring your MOM...
DAD.. SISTER.
BROTHER... KIDS..

to OPEN HOUSE Thursday 16th
from 6 pm. till 8 pm.

VALENTINES PARTY
Friday, Feb 14

BREWED FRESH!
COFFEEHOUSE
an open forum for
theater ~ performance ~ poetry ~ ballads & bits
MATINEE SHOWTIME 2PM
Sunday Feb 16
from 2pm until 6pm
$3
Last Chance for COFFEEHOUSE UNTIL THE NEW CAFE OPENS
SIGN UP NOW! CALL TAMMIE OR BRYAN AT 246-4073
Einstein A Go-Go
327 N 1st ST Jax Bch 249-4646

FILM & MUSIC FEST
****
SUNDAY, JAN 31...OPEN FROM 2 TIL 8PM $4 ALL DAY
3pm...OPEN FEATURE...THE MUMMY
5pm...DANCE MUSIC & VIDEO
****
WEDNESDAY, FEB 3...OPEN FROM 7 TIL 11pm
7pm...MUSIC FEATURE...THE GREAT ROCK N ROLL SWINDLE
****
THURSDAY, FEB 4...OPEN FROM 7 TIL 11pm
DANCE MUSIC & VIDEO
****
FRIDAY, FEB 5....OPEN FROM 7 TIL 1am
ALTERNATIVE MUSIC
****
SATURDAY, FEB 6.....OPEN FROM 7 TIL 1 am
LIVE MUSIC !!!!
10 pm...RIGHT AS RAIN
FROM ATLANTA
****
COMING SOON ..... GALLERY NIGHT....WEDNESDAYS
LOOKING FOR ARTIST TO PARTICIPATE ALL MEDIUMS ...THEATRE PLEASE......
EINSTEIN A GO GO
327 N. 1st ST. , Jax Beach   PH (249-4646)

SUNDAY, FEB. 14
VALENTINES DAY
(BASH)
OPEN 2 & 10 PM
dance music
VIDEO
FILM
fun!
EINSTEIN A GO-GO
327 N 1st ST. Jax Bch

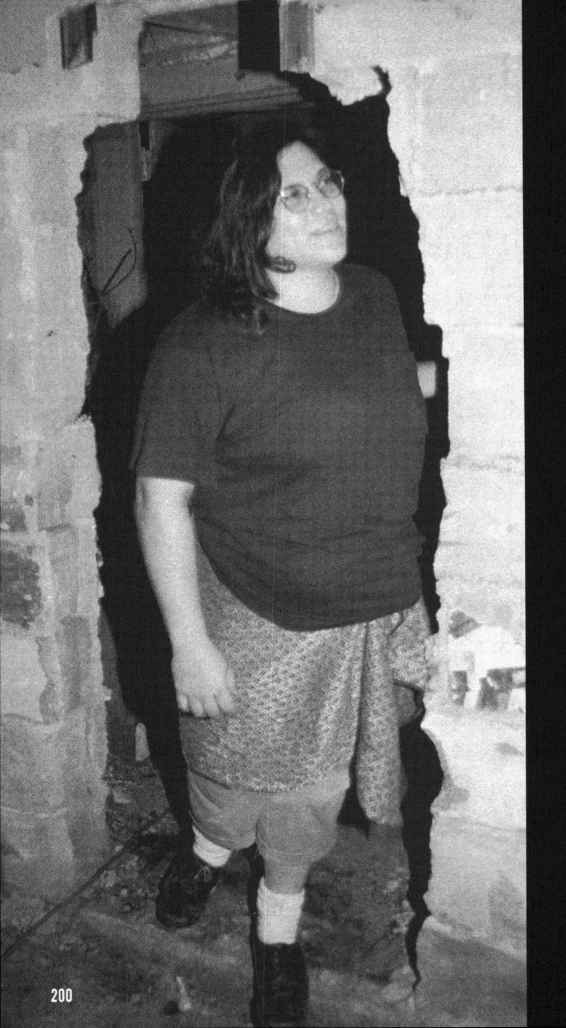

In 1988 the Faircloth family opened a music store called the Theory Shop next door to Einstein's. To connect the two buildings, they literally knocked holes in the walls. For two weeks, people traversed back and forth through the broken cinderblock. The building inspector took one look and said, "No, no, no, no, no, no." The space was then widened to allow for two-way traffic and enclosed with glass blocks.

Theory Shop #12

ANOTHER BRILLIANT IDEA

 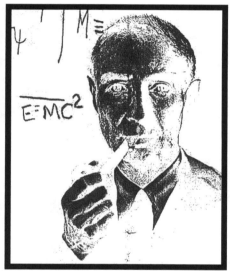 

GRAND OPENING SATURDAY JUNE 18

LOCATED INSIDE EINSTEIN A GO-GO

Hi! It's comin' up to our THIRD YEAR THANKS, FOR SUPPORTING US !! EINSTEIN'S IS CURRENTLY ADDING ON, BY MAY WE WILL HAVE THE THEORY SHOP OPEN. THEORY IS RECORDS, TAPES, T-SHIRTS, CLOTHING, POSTERS AND TON'S O' STUFF. ALSO SUNDAY APRIL 24TH IS THE WILD SWANS RECORD PARTY. FREE RECORDS, TAPES, POSTERS AND VIDEO'S. SPONSORED BY WARNER BROS RECORDS HOPE TO SEE YA SOON!
p.o 49097, Jacksonville

JACKSONVILLE, FL 3
PM
1988

FUCK PARENTAL
ADVICE
SST RECORDS

"The Theory Shop was amazing because the music was so diverse. It hit on so many things. Einstein's led you down the path of music that way and it was very unique."

— Michael Virzera
a.k.a. DJ Dr. Strangelove

THEORY SHOP

"The little store sold records. They also sold sheet music and I remember buying the sheet music to 'Flirtin' with Disaster' by Molly Hatchet. It was something I didn't expect to see, so I bought it and I still have it."

— *Mitch Easter, LET'S ACTIVE*

"My family owned an Abe Livert Record Store when I was growing up, and closed it in '88. When I was finally old enough to go to Einstein's, it was like being back home, flipping through the vinyl and just chilling."

— *Angela Turk*

"There was such an evident family vibe to the place. The elder Faircloths surely provided a parental comfort for many of the kids who had divorced, splintered home lives. Many of us called Connie simply "Mom." When I turned 16, my parents bought me a handful of albums by The Fall, choosing the ones that Tammie recommended. The Faircloths knew their clientele on a deeply personal and arguably now-extinct level that far exceeded customer service. Cultivating relationships seemed to be more crucial to the Faircloths than quick profit."

— DAN BROWN

WORKIN' FOR A LIVIN'

Chuck Kohler

Kristen Morgan

Bryan Massey

Scott Kidd

Marianna Whang

"Funnest job I ever had. I remember the Einstein's crowd was a great group of caring people and I was fortunate enough to have been a small part of that scene."

— *Scott Kidd*

Joe Schaller

"Tammie would ask me to watch the backdoor and make sure people didn't drink in the club. It was pretty funny because you could tell when someone was up to something, so it was just a matter of waiting until they came out of the bathroom and saying, 'Hey, come here for a second,' and smelling their cup. I'd say, 'Where is it?' and turn them over to Tammie or Terri. Then I'd take their booze to the back room and tell the bands to have at it."
— Joel Totty

Mike Whang

Dan Brown

REMEMBER TIPPING IS NOT A CITY IN CHINA!
Jim Howard

"My family lived in Jax Beach, a 15-minute walk from EAGG. I first went to EAGG in 1986 when I was 14 (my first show? Fetchin Bones.) In 1989, Tammie and Terri offered me a job at EAGG. I don't know why since I wasn't a charismatic kid or expressed any interest in working anywhere. Serving Jolt Cola, cleaning ashtrays, mopping up and interacting with musicians like Soundgarden, Dinosaur Jr., Mike Watt and Meat Puppets, helping them unload their gear, watching them soundcheck (including Watt giving me his entire bass guitar and amp history) and more absolutely influenced my decision to record and tour with bands, which I did from ages 20-31. Quite frankly, EAGG in total helped direct my life arc."
— Dan Brown

Chapman Case

Mike Sigil

GAFFERS

CHAPMAN "BELCH" CASE

Seeking big tipper, must like top 40, at least 5 foot 11 and share in freezer space for underwear. Must be able to burp in four foreign languages. Send resume.

JONATHYNE "SUPERMAN" BRIGGS

Likes Wheat Thins, Dr Pepper, Ninja Turtles, wears blue bikini briefs, plays bass and prefers the color green. Looking for Soul-Mate to share in hot vinyl and shower foot farts. Apply in person.

JEREMIAH "GOD" SULLIVAN

Desires Madonna look-alike to join in holy rock band matrimony and eventually get signed to Sub Pop Records. Must be literate. Desperately seeking reply.

TERRI "KARMA" FAIRCLOTH

Club guru searching for nature psychic male. Must like to travel, read Tarot, vegetarian and be kind to animals. Smokers need not to reply. Money not objectionable.

Connie

Terri

Chuck

Kristen

Matt

Emily

Morgan

SPACE AVAILABLE

EINSTEIN A GO-GO

Dedicated to Bill, Connie, Terri and Jeremiah

1985/1991

GAFFERS ARE PEOPLE TOO

JESS "CRAZY LEGS" BOWERS

Seeks Italian women for illicit affair. Must be non-English, good cook, sings well and have large feet to make beautiful wine together. Overseas response hopeful.

TAMMIE "UHM" FAIRCLOTH

Looking for long haired, camal filterless smoking Athens boy for escort to High School reunion. Needs to be able to impress former classmates. Rock Gods a plus. Sex not required.

CHUCK "M.C. MOSES" KOHLER

Once portrayed a orange tree smitten by citrus canker. Looking for perfect women to accompany on Elvis quest. Should be able to rap and is stylin'. Send photo

Wipe your hand across your mouth, and laugh;
The worlds revolve like ancient women
Gathering fuel in vacant lots.

T.S. Eliot

The last word....A note of apology to Jess for the geeky photo (it was the only one I had). Teary farewells to Chapman who is leaving this Summer for U.F. and Jess who will be studying film in Italy. Good luck, we will miss you both. A rather large bunch of daisies to the staff for going beyond the call of duty. Sincere encouragement and good wishes to Terri on her band management endeavor, I'm very proud of you. Internal gratitude to Jeremiah for the helping hand and contribution of the poetry section. For those regular patrons who were not displayed in the contents of this recollection of sorts, I offer vast excuses and apologies. We did not forget you. I would like to thank my mother and father for all their hard work and tolerance, and for making this family of friends complete. We love you. Goodbye to Micheal Huang who is leaving the soundboard for a hip time and fine food in Gainesville. Thanks to Webster's and no thank's to my former English instructors, who as of late seemed to have failed me in my hour of need. To all of those leaving soon we wish you a good life and look forward to your visits.

Love;

Tammie R. Faircloth

206

GOOD FRIENDS, GRATITUDE AND JOLENE

I WAS A WEE 15 YEARS OLD IN THE spring of 1986 when me and my best friend at the time heard about this new "teen club" that opened at the Beaches. During our bus rides to and from Nease High, my soon-to-be best friend Sheila convinced me to go. After talking and talking and talking to my strict parents they agreed to let me go, but only if my friend Dawn went, too. Dawn's older brother, Michael, was kind enough to drive us once he'd critiqued my Go-Go wardrobe — thankfully, I passed!

I was nervous as I walked through the blackened door at Einstein's and saw Jayson, whom I recognized from school, and felt a bit more at ease. He asked me "IS THAT A CLOVE?!" I didn't know what a "clove" was, but I knew I didn't have one so I replied, "No, sorry." I quickly learned what a clove [cigarette] was after being asked for one 14,567 times before I even reached the dance floor! Jakarta brand Cloves became my go-to smokes from Mark's Smoke Shop. (Some of you remember Mark who loved to play chess and would gladly join you in a game before you left the shop.)

I still cherish the many impactful relationships I made back then: Tree Dee, you stayed the night at my house and we used mousse bottles and hairbrushes as microphones as we jumped around singing Siouxsie and Yaz at the top of our lungs. Max, your liberty spikes sure gave my mom something to talk about when she picked us up at the Go-Go when you were staying over, too. We watched *Suburbia* and sat up all night talking. Mom was especially surprised when you woke up with the liberty spikes intact.

During my time at Einstein's I made so many memories with Doug, Allison, Susan, Amy Walker, John, Rodney Jones, Chris Potter and

sooo many more. I remember Fatima and her belly dance, the UFO on the way back from seeing Let's Active in Orlando, and Tickle Pink from Jeanie at The Ritz. Jeanie would card you if you looked 50, but never once carded me. I used to laugh in the liquor store's drive-thru when, after ordering 10-15 bottles, she would simply smile and say, "What a party!" My life was built on all these memories. Thank you all for being such a big part of those formative years and know that I think of you on the regular!

> **Einstein's gave me the soundtrack to my life and a safe place.**

Typically, if you saw your mom walk into a club where you were partying, it would feel like a gut shot. But not at Einstein's. I remember my mom walking through the club with both Tammie and Terri more

Jo Meszaros on the dance floor, 1988

than once. They were genuinely thrilled when a parent showed up to see what the scene was about, more so to make sure their child was safe. I think they enjoyed it when parents cared enough to do that. On nights when my mom was picking me up, she'd watch me dance a while, then call me over to leave.

My first turn on the dance floor was to Strawberry Switchblade's version of "Jolene." I requested that song so many times I think Tammie really started to dislike it. It was very cool when she tracked down several copies (maybe 10) on 12" vinyl and held them for us Jolene-heads. I still have mine.

I worked at the club for a short while, mostly behind the bar, but I also covered the door sometimes and helped Mrs. Connie and Mr. Bill (don't giggle) with whatever they needed behind the scenes for bands and such. Mr. Bill's fried chicken was legendary, but the Faircloth's hospitality went beyond that. I remember seeing these really tired band members, not that much older than me, who seemed to feel at ease when they were at Einstein's on a level I imagine didn't exist for them in many other places.

Einstein's gave me the soundtrack to my life and a safe place, where my looking at other women the way my friends were looking at boys made a little sense since I wasn't alone in that. Knowing early on I wasn't the only one made a HUGE difference in my life and to my confidence. The haven the Faircloths created was a safe space to test the boundaries of what being ourselves meant.

I am eternally grateful to Tammie and the Faircloth family for the space they gave me.

— *Jo Meszaros*

Doing the YMCA
dance,1987

FUN & GAMES

Musical chairs was a popular game that kept things lighthearted

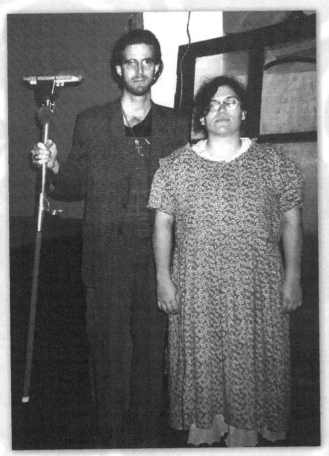

Fred Castor and Tammie: a new American Gothic

 Einstein's always had something
fun going on, including a little
competition every now and then

Sonic Youth joke around with local cable TV personality Willie Idle

one man's trash is another man's treasure

Those Beggar Boys

On the eve of opening for X in 1987, members of the Beggar Weed dressed as beer cans on stage for the club's Halloween show

MORE FUN THAN A Hoot and a HOLLER

Alan Cowart's corset catches the eye of his future wife Michelle

"In 1988 a group of us went to the Athens Music Festival in Georgia. I always had costumes in my trunk because I worked as a singing messenger. During a gas stop Scott Leuthold and Tammie got into the trunk and when I came out of the store they were modeling one of my wigs."

— *Allison Durham*

"Tammie had this trick where she would take rock stars on the beach and throw bread close to their heads so that the seagulls would swoop in. Tammie took [Jane's Addiction's] Perry Farrell out there once. She starts throwing the bread and here come 50 seagulls flying around his head. He started waving his arms as they flew all around him."

— *Shawn Barton Vach*

Living Colour made the most of their visits to Jacksonville Beach

Judy Mareiniss at Jax Beach with Living Colour

"I was sound engineer for Living Colour when we passed through Einstein A Go-Go, fresh out of CBGB and just starting the 1988 tour for *Vivid*. I was struck by how this little joint in Jacksonville looked like it belonged in NYC's East Village. I was taken with the family's kindness. They were homey and even cooked for us! And the club was half a block from the beach! Good times. Good memories. Special place."

— *Judy Mareiniss*

T'S JUST A JUMP TO THE LEFT

INSTEIN'S WOULD SOMETIMES BREAK AWAY from the shoegazing and speaker dancir tracks to play a **waltz**, **"Time Warp"** or **"The Madison."** The first time a waltz blaste cross the dance floor, it was awkward. People typically came to EAGG because they coul lance alone. Plus, who actually knows how to waltz? Terri dismissed the idea saying, ried to do something to bring people together and it just backfired." But the next nigh everal club kids came to her and requested it because they wanted to get close to the crush. After that, the waltz was in the regular rotation.

When Tammie DJed and needed a break from the usual rotation, she would play...

"You Shook Me All Night Long" – AC/DC

"All You Need is Love" – The Beatles

"Guitars, Cadillacs" – Dwight Yoakam

"Atomic Dog" – George Clinton

"Last Train to Clarksville" – The Monkees

"Foxy Lady" – Jimi Hendrix

"Magic Carpet Ride" – Steppenwolf

SAY CHEESE

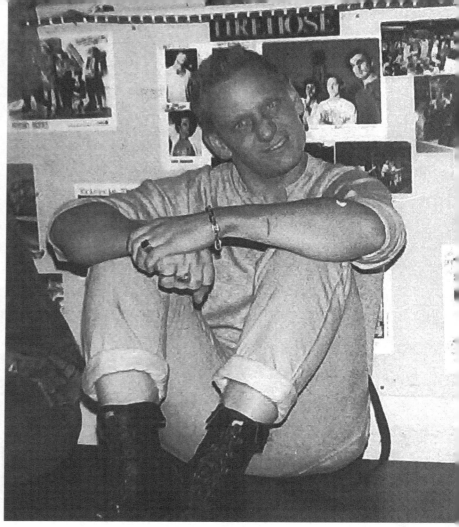

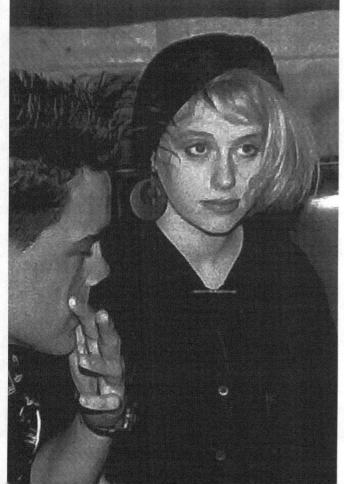

FASHION STATEMENTS

226

"I was 13, so around Fall of '87, my friend Jennifer Breedlove's mom drove us to a show at EAGG. We spent about three hours before picking outfits, which consisted of bits and pieces of each other's clothing. I think I wore a mustard colored baggy turtleneck, black rayon mini skirt, and a giant asymmetrical black belt, with Chinese mary janes. I didn't get to go back very often until Mary Sweisgood-Brisk got her driver's license in May of '89, but I barely missed a night after that!"
—Lori Rebman Shad

BLACKBERRY LIPSTICK FOREVER

THERE WAS A NEVER-ENDING BUZZ swirling around the halls of my high school. Little chats my teenage comrades had about a subversive, underground, perhaps somewhat dangerous club down the street in Jacksonville Beach, called Einstein A Go-Go. I grew up in Ponte Vedra Beach off A1A (an upscale, resort-like area) and had heard rumblings about the club when I entered junior high in 1990. Few of my classmates wouldn't dare even be seen in such a place and I often heard them describe the kids who frequented it as "Steiners." OK, my hometown was more about the PGA Tour, country clubs, beach club memberships, and a twin set of Jaguars in the driveway.

After a seemingly endless summer stuck in summer school taking Personal Fitness before my freshman year — forced to run a mile a day for two weeks straight — I found myself drawn to the older boys in my class. They seemed to know an awful lot about music and had long cheek or chin-grazing '90s grunge hair like Kurt Cobain. Of course, I was all eyes, um, I mean ears.

These soon-to-be seniors were talking about bands I had only shared my love for with my "cool" girlfriends. Bands we'd secretly been listening and choreographing bedroom dances to for the last few years. Bands like The La's, The Sundays, Pixies, Concrete Blonde, and The Charlatans. It wasn't until December that year when my close friend Ally told me, "I went to Einstein's last weekend."

Ally had the cool punk older brother who did "underground" things like skateboard, wear Doc Martens and listen to bands like Sonic Youth. He took her to Einstein A Go-Go and I was incredibly jealous and intrigued. "Um, Einstein's? You mean that club in Jax Beach?" Ally replied, "Yes, it was so much fun! Do

you want to go with me next weekend?" And with that invitation I started planning the hippest outfit possible for a 15-year-old girl in 1992. I could see myself wearing a cute striped vintage 1970s Henley scoop neck top with little white buttons, some black vintage Levi's corduroys, and my new black Nana boots from Edge City. I was all set, and I was finally going to pony up the nerve to go.

Kim Loach in Ponte Vedra Beach, 1993

It was a cold night when Ally and I walked into the small club where a very nice woman was standing there to take our cover charge money. I remember thinking it was friendlier and less scary than some had described it. Sure, it was dark and there was smoke clouding and swirling around the colored lights making the room look like a hazy rainbow. I saw lots of teenagers and young adults dancing near the DJ.

When I first walked in the DJ was playing a song I'd never heard before and

I immediately liked it. "Oh my goodness, who is this?" Now I know it was "Regret" by New Order. Later that night, I heard "Liar" by The Cranberries and had no idea what it was called. That's when I got brave enough to ask DJ Matt Hopkins what the name of the song was.

I think, no I'm positive, I was instantly hooked on the experience — dancing to all those songs, never having had as much fun in my life. It's weird how you can feel at school that you're OK, socially, but then you don't. And that night I knew I'd discovered my people, discovered a place that played the music I loved, especially new wave, alternative and folk. I felt like I'd found a home and I went every weekend after that for about four years.

During the time I went to Einstein's, I was honored to see amazing bands perform and I was lucky enough to see my favorite singer Juliana Hatfield of Blake Babies, in April 1993 during her tour for *Hey Babe*, her phenomenal solo debut. She had amazing bangs, wore a dark cranberry colored lipstick and a glow-in-the-dark horse necklace. I knew all the words to all her songs and might have cried a little when she sang "Here Comes the Pain" and "Ugly." Later, I saw Madder Rose, Fuzzy, Velocity Girl and local stars like Crowsdell. I felt like the luckiest teenage girl alive. I idolized the women in these bands and wanted to be like them, a strong female singer and guitarist. It was everything to me to see these women perform. Without Einstein A Go-Go, it would never have been possible.

In July of 1993, my mother dropped me and my sister off early (as in, we were the ONLY ones there at 6 p.m., way cool) the night of The

Cranberries concert. Because we were so early, the nice ladies who owned EAGG let us come in and hang out, which I thought was so kind, considering the alternative — looking like teen losers sitting on the corner of 1st Street. Best part about it? We got to see what Dolores O'Riordan, lead singer of The Cranberries, bought. Doing my best to not be too much of a lurker, I saw she purchased a Metallica/Guns N' Roses T-shirt (didn't they do some mega-huge double bill stadium tour the year before?) which she ended up wearing that night, while she showed us an authentic Irish jig.

Fast forward, or rewind rather. I'd taken guitar lessons in the 1980s from a few metalheads and thought it was time to pick up my instrument again. My friend was dating a guy she met at EAGG, and he also played guitar and asked me to "jam." Yes, we said "jam" a lot in 1993. That same year we formed Tintern Abbey and subsequently got to perform at Einstein's in 1994 (and later a few more times) with another local outfit, Room 136. It was a great honor to perform on the Einstein's stage, that in my mind was akin to standing on stages at Max's Kansas City or CBGB.

In 1997, Einstein A Go-Go was going to close its doors forever. I had a terrible flu/sinus-infection, but regardless of my poor health, like any 20-year-old girl would, I went and had one last night out, and danced until 2 a.m. The last memory I have of that very last night, was not wanting it to end. To keep dancing to another song, even though my whole body hurt, not from being sick, but from dancing so hard and passionately that night. I remember hearing one of my favorite songs towards the end of the night, "Black Metallic" by Catherine Wheel, and recall standing in the middle of the dance floor with my eyes shut tight, crying. I stood there letting my memories wash over me and,

EINSTEIN A GO-GO
Presents
tintern abbey

Tintern Abbey, 1994: Kim Loach, Terry Brown and Tony Chance

with sadness, wishing the night would never end. All the firsts that happened there: first kiss and subsequent make outs on the beach, making new friends, worshipping alt-rock musicians on stage. But more than anything, all of us growing up together.

> I stood there letting my memories wash over me and, with sadness, wishing the night would never end.

I suppose because I was born at the right time, in the right place, I got to be part of something really special. After Einstein A Go-Go closed I continued to write music and perform. My band ultimately made it

to CBGB around 1998 and we continued to tour in New York City, Philadelphia and Atlanta. I know in my heart that going to Einstein's and being so immersed in alternative music and culture is what made me the woman and mother I am today. I still play in a rock band.

Einstein's was not just a place to go dancing. For me, and probably for a lot of people, it was a place to escape from our high school experiences. It was also a chance to meet kids from other schools, and a place to make friends, dance all night and burn calories, buy the best T-shirts, stickers and new tapes. I had the Theory Shop's red Throwing Muses sticker on my car for years and my older daughter now lives in The Sundays shirt I bought there.

I will be forever grateful and feel a glowing nostalgic love in my heart for everyone I met back then. OK, almost everyone. I was a teenager after all. Revlon Blackberry lipstick forever.

— Kim Loach Floyd

edge city

"Edge City was certainly a huge influence for me back in the late '70s and early '80s. I still walk by in awe of the **house of cool** that Tom and Gunnel built."

— *Tammie Faircloth*

"I had a lot of **baby doll shoes** from Edge City."

— *Denise Reagan*

"I still have all my old **Archaic Smile T-shirts** that I bought at Edge City. Pre-internet Edge City was such a lifeline to an edgier aesthetic out there in the larger world."

— *Patrick Sheehan*

ALTERNATIVE MUSIC REQUIRED alternative fashion and Edge City, a small boutique in Five Points became our favorite destination. Influenced by a punk aesthetic, Gunnel Humphreys and Tom McCleery sold clothes, shoes, jewelry, sunglasses, hair dye, zines, and make-up. The colors were brighter than mainstream fashion, textures were coarser, and the selection of graphic tees featured anything from communist leaders to cats with yarns.

"We had our first **cassette tape** for sale at Edge City."

— *Ian Chase, Rein Sanction*

"I bought my first jar of **Manic Panic** hair dye there. I had fire engine red hair for most of 10 years. When I was 16, I shoplifted a hat from Edge City. I later went to make amends and Tom didn't want to accept the money, even though I made him. Edge City, Five Points and Einstein A Go-Go were my youth. I miss them all."

— *Susie DeFord*

"Tom became **my hero** when I bumped into the fair couple at the 1989 performance of Les Miserables. Tom was in a classic evening suit, a tuxedo, but he had the pants tailored into shorts and was wearing Doc Martens. And Gunnel was in an evening dress that made me sweat when I looked at her."

— Larry Vosmik

"Visits to Edge City helped me clear my brain of all the teenage 'supposed-to-be's' and helped me funk up my wardrobe for the viewing pleasures of my prep school peers. Loved the tunes, the scents and general feelings of acceptance that Tom and Gunnel freely gave all who stepped in. They brought **a little NYC to JAX.** I always left there feeling more empowered and confident to be me with a little kick of weird or crazy. Thank you for your years of inspiration and kindness and faithfulness to all that you both are and were! Legends of Cool!"

— Julie Baggett Kivett

"I used to have quite a few of those Edge City **onion bags**. The hammer and sickle was my favorite because I was into the communist thing at the time. I would collect phone numbers from people I would meet at EAGG every weekend and put them in that bag. It was such an exciting time. I felt accepted."

— Kalani Blakely

"My best friend Coleman and I lived in those vintage European men's **pajama pants**. They were unique and comfortable. I still have at least four pairs and they're a staple of my work-from-home wardrobe."

— Jennifer Curry Compton

"I bought my first article of **Betsey Johnson** at Edge City. It was a pair of black pantaloons with ruffles at the knees. I also bought a black T-shirt with a latex cross and an iron cross in the middle. I spent a whole paycheck! It was so worth it!"

— Beth Hall

"I bought my first pair of Monkey Boots and Doc Martens from Gunnel, circa '88. **Mondo-Creepers** too."

— Travis Julian

1.

2.

3.

4.

TAKE A TOUR

← BACKSTAGE

4.

STAGE

DJ

5.

↰ MAILBOX
for song
requests

DANCE!
2.

Theory Shop

TV

BLEACHERS

SOUND
BOARD

3.

7.

BOYS

6.

GIRLS

THE BAR
Fountain of
Sonic Youth

COUNTER
(stash your stuff here)

ENTER
1.

FIRE
EXIT

5.

6.

7.

232

FREAK SCENE

A selection of photos inside the club after the dust settled

PREVIOUS: Cash register at the front entrance

ABOVE (clockwise): Telephone stand; "Coming Soon" board for fliers; dance floor booth closest to the front entranceway; booth back room with Theory Shop passageway to the left; disco ball light hanging from the ceiling over the dance floor

NEXT: Ashtray in girl's bathroom

Mr. Bill's Famous Fried Chicken Recipe

Here is the recipe for my dad's legendary fried chicken that he cooked for many bands, staff members and anyone else lucky enough to partake. It's been mentioned in magazine interviews and frequently requested on band riders. It may have varied over the years but this was the formula he passed on to me. Please feel free to make it your own.

XOXO Tammie

INGREDIENTS

1 or more whole chicken, skin on, cut up and quartered or up to 8 of your favorite pieces
2   cups vegetable oil
1/8 teaspoon minced garlic, powdered is OK
1/2 teaspoon paprika
1   tablespoon sesame seeds
1   cup self-rising flour, more if needed
Salt and pepper to taste

INSTRUCTIONS

1. Put ingredients into a clean paper grocery bag and mix thoroughly
2. Place chicken into paper bag, close and shake until well coated
3. Pour vegetable oil into electric skillet and heat to 325° F
4. Carefully place chicken in skillet
5. Fry for 10 minutes with no lid, then turn pieces over
6. Fry for 20 minutes with lid on, then turn pieces again
7. Fry for 10 more minutes. Check to see if done. Larger pieces may take longer
8. Place chicken on a plate lined with paper towels and serve!

The End Is Here

The Final Weekend

Thursday 8-12 $3

Friday 8-2 $4

Saturday Late Night at the Go-Go **8-4** $5

Sunday *Coffeehouse/Art Show* **2-6** $2

Last Night!

Sunday 8-2 $4

Einstein A Go-Go would like to Thank Everyone for all of their Love and Support over the past 12 years. We are very sad to see the doors of this incredible, infamous, nightclub shut forever. It has meant so much to so many people. But, the time has come to move on to different adventures, new experiences, starting over and creating a new World. The Faircloth Family will be starting a new venture with a coffe bar/cafe where we will continue doing Coffeehouse, live Music and the occasional dance night.
You can call 249-4646 for updates on this exciting new project.

We hope to see you once again in the new Millenium!

SIGN OUR MAILING LIST TO KEEP IN TOUCH AND TO FIND OUT ABOUT EXCITING UP-COMING PROJECTS FROM EINSTEIN A GO-GO. INCLUDING VIDEOS OF SOME OF THE FAMOUS BANDS THAT HAVE PLAYED THERE, A COMPLETE BOOK ON THE GO-GO, A WEB PAGE, AND MERCHANDISING SURE TO KEEP THE NAME OF EINSTEIN A GO-GO ALIVE.

EINSTEIN A GO-GO
1985-1997

"I was in tech school in the Air Force when Einstein's closed. My mom sent me the newspaper article with the picture of the big Einstein's sign. I sat on my bed and cried when I read it."
— *Mary Donovan*

"I had maybe a week's notice. Tammie gave a heartfelt speech about the club in her Tammie Faircloth way. She said, **'For the last song I've decided to have silence. I just want us to get together on the floor and talk to each other one more time before we have to leave.'**"

— *Ricky Hattaway*

"It was kind of surreal in ways because we had gone there for so long. I don't remember a true feeling that it was closing until after the last night when we started to move things out of there. That's when it really sunk in."

— *Becky Gibson*

"We decided to close because alternative music had became more popular, other clubs were opening and the beach itself was changing with new development. When it closed I remember sitting on the roof with Tammie just looking at the stars and we agreed it was a good run. And now it's done."

— *Terri Faircloth*

"My best friend Leah carved out a piece of the dance floor for me after Einstein's closed when we were helping with the move."

— *Melody White-Crinon*

THE LONG DRIVE HOME

"Arlington wasn't exactly far, but we always waited until the very last minute to leave and then had to race up Girvin to try and make curfew. Why did they always play the BEST songs when it was time to go?"

— *Kim Barrows*

"I drove down from Georgia. If I didn't crash on someone's couch in Jax I had to pull over in Kingsland to sleep for an hour. Woke up one morning to a police officer tapping on my window. I had fallen asleep in a hotel parking lot with my lights still on. Luckily my battery wasn't dead and I drove home."

— *Gary C. Daniels*

"Back then there was nothing on J. Turner Butler Boulevard. It went all the way down to Philips Highway with not that many exits or cops around. At that hour I would go 80-90 mph. It was probably not the best decision for a 16-year-old driver, but I was always in a rush to make it home by curfew. I rarely made it, so not only did I have to race home as fast I could, but then I would have to sneak in as quietly as possible."

— *Jenny Thomas Medure*

"We drove from Orange Park. Didn't mind the drive. My only problem was I would get these terrible foot cramps all the time somewhere on JTB. It was a combination of dancing all night in those karate slipper shoes from Edge City and driving a manual transmission. Inevitably, I would have to stop the car and get out to hop around and stretch my foot. Just part of the fun. "

— *Jennifer Zelenka LaSala*

"I drove to and from Orange Park at least three times a week. Never regretted it once."

— *Matt Brink*

"Maybe your crush was at the club and maybe you didn't say anything to them, or maybe they gave you a signal or some shit. You just had a lot of stuff to think about on that long drive home."

— *Chris Mondia*

"At 2 a.m., I'd have to decide if I wanted to try and make the drive home to Fernandina Beach or crash on a friend's couch closer to the club. I almost always drove home and usually regretted it: dark, empty roads, lots of deer and fear that I'd succumb to the overwhelming urge for sleep. When I moved to Jacksonville and befriended Tammie and Terri, we would close at 2 and sweep up the club before heading to the Philips Mall to dance at a gay club until 5 in the morning. Those nights ended with an early breakfast at Village Inn before the race to make it home before the sunrise — just like a vampire."

— ALLISON DURHAM

"I still remember my drive home on JTB the last night they were open because it was at sunrise. I will never forget that sad drive home. I still have the best friends of my life from those times. We are so special to have experienced such a time and place and music."

— *Amanda Smith Hiers*

A LASTING LEGACY

Einstein A Go-Go played a significant part in shaping the lives of so many who walked through its doors between 1985 and 1997. The club lives on in spirit and memories and is still dearly missed decades later.

10,000 MANIACS continue to record and perform with Mary Ramsey on lead vocals. Natalie Merchant has had a very successful career as a solo artist with nine albums so far and regular tours.

ALEKA'S ATTIC recorded several songs before River Phoenix's death in 1993 that have appeared online and in films, however, an official album of the band's material has yet to be released.

Tammie Faircloth and Scott Leuthold at Beggar Weeds' show at Rain Dogs in Jax, 2023

BEGGAR WEEDS reunite for live shows regularly and through Strolling Bones Records will issue previously unreleased songs recorded with R.E.M.'s Michael Stipe in 1991, plus a new record in the near future.

Martin Atkins of **BRIAN BRAIN** is a music industry author and university instructor, plus founder of the Museum of Post-Punk and Industrial Music in Chicago.

BUFFALO TOM released their 11th album, *Jump Rope*, in 2024 and remain a live favorite in Boston and beyond.

CAMPER VAN BEETHOVEN founder David Lowery leads alt-rock favorites Cracker and David Immerglück plays with Counting Crows, while Victor Krummenacher and Jonathan Segal have released numerous solo projects and film scores. CVB mini-reunion gigs still happen, too.

JIM CARROLL garnered attention for the 1995 movie based on his autobiography *The Basketball Diaries* starring Leonardo DiCaprio and continued writing until his death in 2009.

Chickasaw Mudd Puppies with pal Scott Leuthold, 2024

CHICKASAW MUDD PUPPIES re-emerged from a three-decade recording hiatus in 2023 with the release of *Fall Line* that enlisted Beggar Weeds drummer Alan Cowart on the skins.

ALEX CHILTON is revered as one of rock's greatest songwriters for his work with Big Star and as a solo artist prior to his death in 2010. The Replacements had it right all along.

Common Thread at Sun Ray Cinema in Jax, 2024

COMMON THREAD released a 30th anniversary edition of their 1993 LP *Fountain* on Fort Lowell Records and reunited for a Jacksonville performance at Sun Ray Cinema's Sleeping Giant film festival in 2024.

The Connells at Intuition Ale Works in Jax, 2022

THE CONNELLS recorded nine albums with their latest, *Steadman's Wake*, released in 2021 prompting shows up and down the East Coast including Jacksonville.

THE CRANBERRIES enjoyed tremendous commercial and critical success selling more than 40 million albums worldwide before the tragic passing of lead singer Dolores O'Riordan in 2018.

Shannon Wright emerged from **CROWSDELL** to become a critically acclaimed singer-songwriter, releasing several albums with Touch and Go/ Quarterstick records and recording with famed producer Steve Albini.

The dB'S original members found their way back to each other for a 2024 tour coinciding with the re-issue of their debut album on Propeller Sound Recordings.

THE DEAD MILKMEN reunited after a 13-year break in 2008, releasing several more of their satirical punk albums including *Quaker City Quiet Pills* in 2023.

DINOSAUR JR.'s original lineup of J Mascis, Lou Barlow and Murph reformed in 2005 and still crank out their fuzzy noise rock live and in the studio along with numerous solo releases.

DRIVIN N CRYIN joined the Georgia Music Hall of Fame in 2015 and are road warriors to this day with dozens of shows annually.

FAITH NO MORE's on-again, off-again status with sporadic albums and tours has quieted in recent years while Mike Patton and other members work on various projects.

Hope and Aaron of Fetchin Bones performing with It's Snakes at Ciné in Athens, 2023

FETCHIN BONES recorded and toured with the likes of R.E.M., The B-52s and Red Hot Chili Peppers until 1990. Since then, Hope Nicholls and Aaron Pitkin played with Sugarsmack and It's Snakes, and Errol Stewart helped remaster unearthed Fetchin Bones demos in 2020. They were inducted into the North Carolina Music Hall of Fame in 2023.

Mike Watt, 2022

fIREHOSE produced five albums and toured non-stop before disbanding in 1994. Mike Watt, George Hurley and Ed Crawford have found homes with other bands and projects including Watt's stints with J Mascis and the Fog and Pornos for Pyros. They reunited for 14 shows in 2012 including the Coachella music festival.

FISHBONE never stopped performing or recording their brand of ska, punk and funk with original members Angelo Moore and Christopher Dowd still leading the band's charge.

The Flaming Lips at Florida Theatre in Jax, 2024

THE FLAMING LIPS have won three Grammy Awards, and in 2002 were on *Q* magazine's list of "50 Bands to See Before You Die." With 16 albums, the Lips continue to deliver eye-popping live spectacles at their concerts.

ROBYN HITCHCOCK's creative endeavors have never slowed as a performer, poet or painter. In 2024, Robyn released his memoir, *1967: How I Got There and Why I Never Left*.

HUGO LARGO disbanded in 1991 with vocalist Mimi Goese going on to collaborate with the likes of Moby and Tim Sommer joining MTV as an on-air correspondent. A collection of Hugo Largo's live and unreleased tracks was slated for a 2024 release.

INDIGO GIRLS have enjoyed wide-ranging success and continue to tour. They won the 2022 Spirit of Americana/Free Speech Award and found rekindled interest in 2023 thanks to a prominent spot for their hit "Closer to Fine" in the blockbuster *Barbie* movie.

JANE'S ADDICTION are still active and regarded as one of alternative music's most influential acts. Lead singer Perry Ferrell launched the Lollapalooza music festival, which has since expanded into eight territories around the world.

KILKENNY CATS reunited for their first show since 1991 at their hometown AthFest 2024 and are preparing re-releases of their original albums on Propeller Sound Recordings.

Since 1981, Mitch Easter of **LET'S ACTIVE** has produced, engineered and contributed to albums from dozens of recording artists including The dB's, Polvo and Drive-By Truckers. Easter was inducted into the North Carolina Music Hall of Fame in 2016.

Corey Glover, Living Colour in Atlanta, 2024

KEEP DANCING

Former beach kid rickoLus found his haven at Einstein's

Rick Colado, 1995

JACKSONVILLE BEACH'S Rick Colado first gigs as a teen at Einstein's led to a formidable fan base for The Julius Airwave and then several albums and EPs under his solo moniker, rickoLus. His 2021 album, *Bones*, included his upbeat ode to nights on 1st Street.

"This song is talking about my experience being a beach kid who found Einstein's. There were always the dudes cruising by with their booming cars yelling 'freaks' and other shit at us. There's a bunch of band and song references in there such as the first song I ever remember dancing to, Adorable's 'Homeboy.' As for Ride's 'Vapour Trail,' I have a vivid memory of getting to the club early right after the doors opened. I was walking through to the Theory Shop and that song was playing just as the smoke machines were heating up."
— *Rick Colado, rickoLus*

rickoLus, 2024

Keep Dancing

they came out to fight
those good ol' boys in their boom cars
but we had the right
to dance all night at the go-go bar
we were just kids
the world was so wild and big
break my skateboard on a skinhead
it was survival down on first street,
she said

Hey!
we're only dancing
gonna keep on dancing
we're gonna keep on dancing

you didn't want to go home
your mom was drunk and your
dad was alone
but your sister left you an Unrest
record and a little pipe
the metalheads with their poison hair
stumble out on the boardwalk in
their snake-skin pants
they beat their fading era out on you
they're just jocks in make-up
that don't know what to do

Hey!

we're only dancing
we're gonna keep on dancing
we're gonna keep on dancing

guitar!

hey little girl with the vapor trail
I wish I could be your homeboy
ride my bike through the golf course
at night
just a poor kid living a rich kids life
they shut the doors back in '96
and the music died down on first street

we all grew up and we all got lost
but I still hear those songs inside of me

dancing dancing yeah
we're gonna keep on dancing
we're gonna keep on dancing
we're gonna keep on dancing

LIVING COLOUR achieved international fame before breaking up in 1995 and then reforming in 2000. With Corey Glover ranked among *Billboard*'s "Greatest Rock Lead Singers of All Time" and Vernon Reid among *Rolling Stone*'s "Top 250 Greatest Guitarists," the band remains a popular touring act.

Armistead Wellford of Love Tractor, 2024

LOVE TRACTOR are in the midst of reissuing their original albums and were honored with a plaque on the Athens Music Walk of Fame in 2022.

MIRACLE LEGION reunited in 2024 for a string of shows to accompany the re-release of their first album, *Surprise, Surprise, Surprise*. Singer Mark Mulcahy's side project Polaris was the house band for the TV show *The Adventures of Pete & Pete*.

MODERN ENGLISH's classic "I Melt With You" continues to draw fans to the band's live shows including the 2023 Cruel World music festival in California.

MUDHONEY maintain their place atop Sub Pop's roster, having released eight albums with the storied Seattle label including 2023's *Plastic Eternity*.

MY LIFE WITH THE THRILL KILL KULT has continued to record and tour with a rotating lineup and has contributed songs to the soundtracks of several movies.

NIRVANA will forever be synonymous with grunge music and Kurt Cobain seen as its messiah. Since the frontman's 1994 death, bassist Krist Novoselic has championed social causes when not playing in assorted musical projects while drummer Dave Grohl's Foo Fighters have become one of modern rock's most successful acts.

MOJO NIXON, the self-described "libertarian cynicalist anarchrist," continued to perform and hosted several shows for Sirius Satellite Radio. He passed away in 2024 while on the Outlaw Country Cruise.

Larry Tee, 2022

Larry Tee of **NOW EXPLOSION** is a Berlin-based music producer and DJ who curated the 2001 Electroclash Festival in New York that coined the dance genre's name for acts that blended new wave synth-pop with techno and EDM.

Frank Orrall of **POI DOG PONDERING** juggles plenty as the touring percussionist for Thievery Corporation, private chef and author of an upcoming trilogy of books that will be a retrospective of Poi Dog Pondering's 40-year history.

PRIMUS has consistently toured behind and between their albums with all three original members active in side projects, including bassist Les Claypool's Frog Brigade and drummer Tim "Herb" Alexander's work with A Perfect Circle and Puscifer.

Pylon Reenactment Society at Ciné in Athens, 2023

PYLON was honored in 2020 by their hometown as one of the original inductees of the Athens Music Walk of Fame. Founding member Vanessa Briscoe Hay fronts the band's spiritual successor, Pylon Reenactment Society, which released *Magnet Factory* in 2024.

RED HOT CHILI PEPPERS reached well into the stratosphere and are considered one of the best-selling rock bands of all time. The six-time Grammy winners were inducted into the Rock & Roll Hall of Fame in 2012.

REIN SANCTION's revival has Brannon and Mark Gentry once again performing the scuzzy psychedelic blues rock that drew the attention of Sub Pop three decades ago.

THREE GIRLS

Laura Minor's poetic tribute to her Einstein's nights from her 2024 collection, Bright Life, Animal Heart

"When you are young, music and movement are your gods. I still believe it was one of the most thrilling times of our lives. I just wanted us to remember that in some reconciled way. To be that free on a dance floor was everything, and I hope all of us EAGGers still make time to move to the music we still need."

— *Laura Minor*

The Three Girls:
Cadra Culley, Laura Minor
and Ama Reynolds, 1992

Three Girls

O to be on a dance floor
filled again, mascara with tequila,
*   hair in speaker,*
clovered crowns, snatched cosmos—
save us now

as we round our bodies
into more sensible clothes
sensible houses—
*   no dancing in sight.*

What is it about a girl
*   with a license to break open the earth?*
We could have thrown men to the gators,
*   drove dogs to Canada.*

When we move now,
*   it's alone,*
forever glommed,
the divine bass as laughter
*   reignited in the great diagram.*

Tommy
Stinson,
2024

THE REPLACEMENTS' notoriously unpredictable, alcohol-fueled live shows remain etched in alternative music lore long after the band's initial 1991 break-up. Along with a 'Mats reunion from 2012-2015, Paul Westerberg gained acclaim for his solo work, Tommy Stinson played with Guns N' Roses for more than a decade and Chris Mars found his calling as a painter.

HENRY ROLLINS parlayed his early musical and spoken-word experience into a high-profile career as a media figure regularly appearing on TV, radio and podcasts.

SCREAMING TREES achieved critical acclaim and commercial success as pioneers of Seattle's grunge scene until breaking up in 2000. Mark Lanegan died in 2022 and Van Conner in 2023.

SONIC YOUTH embraced their role as alternative music's godparents, cited as an influence by the likes of Pavement, Ride, Slowdive and many others. The band's 30 years together ended in 2011 with all members continuing as the drivers of experimental music.

SOUL ASYLUM founder Dave Pirner keeps the band in the studio and on the road. Bassist Karl Mueller died of throat cancer in 2005, and the band works with Kill Kancer, a non-profit started by Mueller's widow.

SUPERCHUNK actively tours and records as well as champions today's indie rock through Laura Ballance and Mac McCaughan's Merge Records, which celebrated its 35th anniversary in 2024.

THEY MIGHT BE GIANTS' popularity as a musical act for all ages has resulted in nearly two dozen albums, including several specifically for children.

VIOLENT FEMMES remain celebrated by fans of their folk-punk music and toured for the 40th anniversaries of their classic self-titled debut and *Hallowed Ground*.

WEEN took a break from their offbeat brand of music for three years before reuniting in 2015 and releasing their first new song, "Junkie Boy," in more than a decade in 2024.

X announced their final album, *Smoke & Fiction*, and tour in 2024 featuring all four original members: Exene Cervenka, John Doe, Billy Zoom and DJ Bonebrake.

FRIDAY NIGHT AT EINSTEIN'S

Getting lost in the music is all Tracy Shedd wanted to do

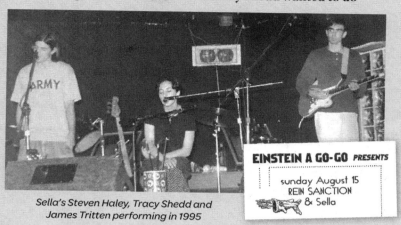

Sella's Steven Haley, Tracy Shedd and James Tritten performing in 1995

EINSTEIN A GO-GO *PRESENTS*

sunday August 15
REIN SANCTION
& Sella

TRACY SHEDD NEVER SHIED AWAY FROM A CHALLENGE — especially with a recording session and coveted Einstein's slot on the line. Her band at the time, Sella, was in the midst of shuffling members leaving them without a guitarist or primary songwriter. Having a guitar she had yet to learn to play, Tracy taught herself in two weeks in order to record the group's next EP and grace the Einstein stage as Sella's newest incarnation. That pivotal point seeded Sella's musical success locally before the act adopted her moniker and moved to Boston.

There she met Teen-Beat Records founder Mark Robinson who released her initial albums on the heralded indie label. The buzz around her songwriting would launch cross-country tours —including one with Sonic Youth's Steve Shelly on drums — and would land her music on shows like *Dawson's Creek* and *One Tree Hill*. On 2013's *Arizona*, Tracy tried to paint the picture of "Friday Night at Einstein's."

"It's later in the night, and the DJ's mailbox is literally full," Tracy explains. "You can see your request is not going to get played — unless you're dating the DJ or something. So you just end up being like, 'I just want to have a good time.' There will always be some good songs to dance to with your friends who will be out there, too, and just get lost in the music."

Tracy and her husband James Tritten (of Tumblewēd and Sella, too) have tapped into the spirit Einstein's instilled in them with Fort Lowell Records that features a deep roster of indie musicians and as hosts of vinyl dance nights in their homebase of Wilmington, North Carolina.

"Every time I was there, I felt like we were so lucky," Tracy says. "I never took it for granted, and that's why I had a meltdown when it closed. Even though I was older myself, we needed Einstein's. The youth needed it."

Tracy Shedd circa 1995 at Village Inn, a favorite after-hours spot

Friday Night at Einstein's

I'm spinning around in a corner

Just spinning around and I'm waiting on you

You're sitting there in a corner head way down low waiting on me

And I'm dancing to whatever comes on

Yeah we're dancing and we don't know this song, but everybody's singing along

The DJ box is full

I guess I'll dance to something not cool

And I'll close my eyes and pretend I'm dancing with you

And I'm dancing to whatever comes on

Yeah we're dancing and we don't know this song, but everybody's singing along

REUNIONS

BACK TOGETHER

An Einstein's-themed concert at Fuel Coffeehouse in Five Points in 2006 brought enthusiastic fans together for a night featuring Beggar Weeds, Holopaw, Tony Rojas and Shawn Barton.

OPHS/EAGG 20ISH REUNION

In 2011, Orange Park 'Steiners got together in the restaurant/bar that took over the old EAGG space at 327 N. 1st Street

ORANGE PARK HIGH SCHOOL'S class of 1991 was having its 20th reunion in 2011. There was a Facebook group for the event and it was filled with bickering, which resulted in two different events being planned. Watching the drama unfold I realized I didn't care much about attending either one. As a teen I'd hoped there would be an Einstein's reunion when I was older, so instead of going to one for my high school class I decided to plan a reunion for all the Orange Park High progressive/alternative/goth/skater/weirdo/artistic/didn't-quite-fit-in kids that I'd hung out with. So many of my friends that had carpooled to the Go-Go on weekends were from different graduation classes, so we opened it up to classes from '89-'92.

Where else could it be held but Einstein's?! Coleman Kane and I went to the former location, which had become Fionn MacCool's, to check it out. They had turned the upstairs into a private area with its own bar. I rented the space, planned a menu, and got to work on invites, postcards, buttons, magnets, and keychains while Coleman created a playlist for the night. We even put the music on flash drives for people to take home along with other souvenirs.

The OPHS/EAGG 20ish Reunion had about 50 attendees. People came from as far away as Thailand, as well as California and Massachusetts. I brought my photo booth and we took so many awesome pictures. We had dinner, drinks, a little dancing, and a lot of talking. When the restaurant closed at 2 a.m. about 25 to 30 of us went to the hotel next door, where a lot of us were staying, and continued the party. I remember the entire room doing "The Time Warp" at some point. It was one of the most fun nights of my adult life and I still can't believe we didn't have the front desk called on us.

— *Kristen Morgan*

Fionn MacCool's at the former EAGG location

"So many thanks and so much love to Tammie and the Faircloth family for giving us a home back then — a place where we felt comfortable and safe, a club filled with music, laughter and friends that we loved more than some of our own families. Once I started working there, all those feelings increased tenfold. Some of the greatest memories of my life happened at EAGG and because of EAGG. There just aren't enough words to explain what Einstein's means to me."

— *Kristen Morgan*

REUNION PARTY

SAT JULY 26 / 8 PM
$10 COVER

ECLIPSE 4219 St Johns Ave Jacksonville, Florida

AN EPIC DANCE PARTY

EINSTEIN'S REGULARS SCATTERED TO THE WIND AFTER 1997 until like so many things in life, they reunited through the internet. In 2008, Dee Edenfield Marling started an Einstein A Go-Go group page on Facebook. She hoped others would be eager to share their memories. For years the word "reunion" floated around and in 2014 a reunion party was held at Eclipse in Riverside. Four hundred people danced to the soundtrack of their youth and reconnected with lost friends. Some waited in line to tell Tammie how much the club meant to them, thanking her for a safe place with awesome music. Then, for years afterwards the word "book" floated around.

"I feel like there's so many things you can trace back to the Faircloth family having the music store first, and then The Music Shop, and then the club. So many people were affected by that and loved it. Then they grew up and shared it with their families."

— Christian Mendez

"One hundred percent, there is not an ounce of doubt in my mind, I would not be the person I am today, I would not have gotten into music, I would not have toured the world, I would not be pressing records today. It's a hundred percent because I went to Einstein's."

— CASH CARTER

The epic dance party reunion
at Eclipse in 2014

EINSTEIN a GO-GO
327 N. 1st ST.

FUNDRAISER FOR RIVER PHOENIX CENTER FOR PEACE

Thank You!

THIRD ANNUAL EAGG REUNION PARTY!
PORTION OF PROCEEDS TO BENEFIT SAVANNAH GOODMAN'S MEDICAL AND RECOVERY ESPENSES

Saturday, Sept 24th @ Eclipse

WITH DJ RICKY HATTAWAY

THIRTY A GO-GO

In 2015, DJ Ricky Hattaway returned to Eclipse for a 30-year Einstein's reunion where all those in attendance got to revel in nostalgia, old friendships, and enough '80s/90s tunes to keep everyone moving like the good old days.

LIKE A TEENAGER AGAIN, I was totally stoked when Tammie gave me her blessing to work on an Einstein A Go-Go reunion party. It took awhile to convince her until she suggested that I team up with Dee Edenfield Marling and Allison Durham to make it happen. I couldn't believe I'd have the opportunity to bring Einstein's back for a night.

We had a blast, and it wound up being three years of reunion parties at Eclipse nightclub, Black Sheep restaurant and Rain Dogs bar that brought together that amazing group of people again. The '80s and '90s Einstein's kids got to know each other

Allison Durham, Tammie Faircloth, Andrew Paul Williams and Dee Edenfield Marling

as adults, new friendships were formed, and many meaningful reconnections occurred.

In bringing this fun, eclectic crowd together again, I was struck by how everyone who frequented the club thought it was "their" place, and I think that says a lot about what the Faricloths created in that space and time. The positive impact EAGG has had on many areas of our lives made it really meaningful to celebrate it and each other.

Having clubgoers, friends from Edge City and Debrah's, DJs from different eras and Tammie with merch like The Music Shop and Einstein Kitsch Inn days all there brought back that feeling of being a part of the epic scene and original spirit the Faircloths created. Seeing the impact Tammie and her family had on all of us, and dancing to the most incredible music again was something I felt proud and grateful to have worked on.

— *Andrew Paul Williams*

WITH CONSTANT REQUESTS for the ever-popular Einstein A Go-Go T-shirts, Tammie Faircloth created the EAGGheads pop-up shop in 2021. Set at Native Sun Natural Food Market in Jacksonville Beach, the event turned into a mini-reunion with music by DJ Ricky Hattaway, a live set by rickoLus and an auction during which bidding got competitive for vintage tees and more.

"If I hadn't grown up in Jacksonville with access to Einstein's I don't think I would have a sliver of the knowledge I have now about music. I found out about The Jesus and Mary Chain by going to Einstein's and I am now the publicist for them."

— DANIEL GILL

Einstein a Go-Go

"EAGG was the safe place where I could go and be myself. It helped me learn who I was, who I am."
— Kelly Gerganous

"There are things I would have never known about in Jacksonville had I not met the people there. When you grew up in a redneck town and the best part of Rock 105 was the 'Get the Led Out,' having Einstein's really broadened our horizons."
— Chris Tomaski

"It changed my life for sure. It shaped my whole music idea. When people ask me 'How did you find these bands?' I found them because of Einstein's."
— Emily Wilder

"I came out there because I felt so comfortable and accepted."
— Rebecca Brillhart

"I wonder what kind of person I might have been if I hadn't felt a part of that world, and didn't long to find a place that gave me that same feeling in adulthood."
— Christopher Hooker

"I am fortunate in that my father has always loved music and passed that passion to me. But it was my time at EAGG that helped me form my own taste and forged my love for live music in particular. At 50, I still go see live music regularly and can't imagine my life without it. I'm so grateful for my years at EAGG and only wish my 17-year-old daughter had a place that special. There was nothing else like it."
— Vanessa Howren Reid

"I always felt like I didn't fit in. We moved several times when I was young, and while I had many acquaintances, I had few true friends that understood me. That changed when I went to Einstein's. I may not have been as cool as the other kids there (I was dressed more like Belinda Carlisle than Siouxsie Sioux), but I loved the music, the energy and the scene unfolding around me. I had never been in a situation where I wasn't worried that people were judging me. I sat at a table at Einstein's with a guy (soon to be my ex) and he refused to mingle. I got up and danced by myself and I did not care what he or anyone else thought. It was a liberating feeling — to be myself for a song, an hour, a night. I still dance in the same dorky way and I still love live music. I made so many friends over the years who share the same passion for music. Einstein's sparked that joy for me."

— Siobhan White

"The first time I went to EAGG I had terrible social anxiety. As I walked up to the door 'Go!' by Tones on Tail was playing. The lyrics are all about getting over your fears and getting out there to enjoy life. I still listen to it 35 years later when I need some positive motivation."

— Scott Erickson

"The music literally saved my life."
— Jayson John Evans

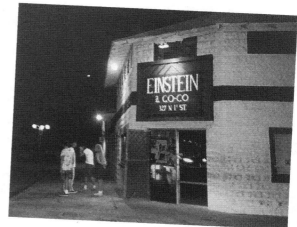

"I feel that we're so lucky to have had such a unique thing right here in freaking Jacksonville — something that artistic, something that avant garde. And it wasn't for drugs, it wasn't for alcohol. The kids were there for the fucking music. It was really all about the music. It almost makes me cry because you don't have that anymore. That's our little part of history here in Jacksonville and it blows my mind. I love it. I'm so proud of that place."

— Ryan Turk

"Einstein's provided an example of how to be a human being. It changed me fundamentally because it changed the way I look at the world and the way I look at people that are different. If it wasn't for that place my life would be a lot different. "
— Tony Rojas

"EAGG taught me about perception and legend. Hundreds of people claim to have seen Nirvana there. In reality, that night they sounded lackluster and played to a smaller audience. People want to be within legends, and EAGG was the flashpoint for those kinds of shared experiences, even ersatz claims and unreal narratives. I find this fascinating."

— Dan Brown

"Einstein's was a safe haven for me. Coming from a chaotic home life, it offered community with fellow music-loving creatives. It changed my life for the better. I felt seen and safe. Thanks to Tammie and family."
— Catina Jane Stover Gray

Ralph Williams, 1989

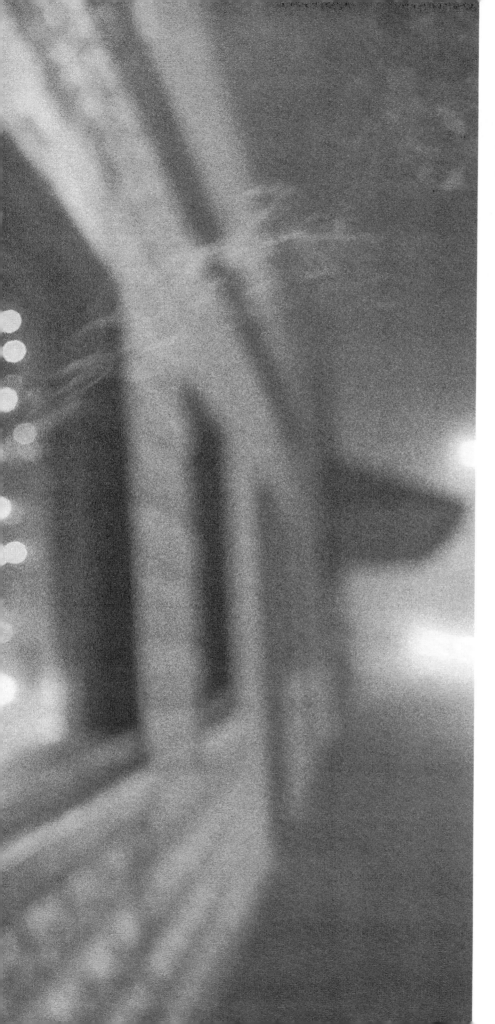

IN MEMORIUM

Our Einstein's friends and musicians who are no longer with us. Rest in Peace.

Bill & Connie Faircloth ♥
Keli Aydlotte
Melissa Ball
Randy Bewley *Pylon*
Jance Brown *Chompfish*
Dell Burks
Jim Carroll
Laura Carter *Bar-B-Q Killers*
Alex Chilton
Rob Clayton *The Jody Grind*
Kurt Cobain *Nirvana*
Van Conner *Screaming Trees*
Matt "Coop" Cooper
Matt Cooper
Chris Cornell *Soundgarden*
Thomas Davis
Peter Enriquez *Fin Fang Foom*
Robert Hayes *The Jody Grind*
Brian Hicks *Gizzard*
Faye Hunter *Let's Active*
Brian Jerin
Russ Kennington *Chompfish*
Anne Knowles
Jonathan LaPrade
Deacon Lunchbox
Mark Lanegan *Screaming Trees*
Judy Mareiniss *Sound Engineer*
"Joberre" Markwordt
Steve Mason *Bell Book and Candle*
Chris McFall *Big Velvet Elvis, et al*
Ray McKelvey *"Stevie Stilletto"*
Karl Mueller *Soul Asylum*
Mojo Nixon
Dolores O'Riordan *The Cranberries*
River Phoenix *Aleka's Attic*
Dexter Romwebber *The Flat Duo Jets*
Sara Romwebber *Let's Active*
Hillel Slovak *Red Hot Chili Peppers*
Tim Starr *Pretty Boy Freud*
Christopher Stesen
Dave This *Lazzaroni*
Geordie Walker *Killing Joke*
Jeff Walls *Guadalcanal Diary*
Ralph Williams
Ben Wright
Jim Youngman
Joey Zimmerman *Common Thread*

"I was lucky to play at Einstein A Go-Go after attending many shows there in the '80s: 10,000 Maniacs, Pylon, Love Tractor, Guadalcanal Diary, Naomi's Hair, Chickasaw Mudd Puppies, Beggar Weeds and too many more to name. This photo is of my band One Minute Father playing the venue in 1986. No, you've never heard of us. We unceremoniously disbanded when a fellow band member became an addict, stole some of my equipment and left town. But, I had a life-changing moment that night. After our set, Terri Faircloth, who was running sound, approached me and said, 'You guys are great! You're better than most of the out-of-town bands we book!' I had low self-esteem at the time and those few simple words changed my whole life. I would later go on to be in two South Florida bands: dogs on ice (Allied Records) and my eponymous band, Joe Popp (Space 44). These bands both released multiple recordings and opened for Green Day, Blink 182, Mike Watt, Joan Jett & the Blackhearts and Cheap Trick. Thank you Terri and the Einstein's community for so many great shows and the boost a young guy needed to help him find his way."

— Joe Popp

CONTRIBUTERS

Michael J. Allen   ROBERT ARMSTRONG   Emily Augustus Westergaard   CLARA BATTON SMITH   Sherry Beadle   JENNIFER BENdETTI
HAYLEY BIERMAN   Zachary Boyle   JESS BOWERS   JONATHYNE BRIGGS   VANESSA BRISCOE HAY   Ron Burman   JASON BUSCH
Craig Campbell   WENDY CAMPBELL   Cary Cantor-Walz   Cash Carter   Zak Champagne   IAN CHASE   Danny C. Chavis
JOM CHEEK   Happy Chichester   MARK CLINE   MARY COBB   Rick Colado   MIKE CONNELL   GARY LEE CONNER   CRUCIAL EDDY COTTON
Alan Cowart   PHIL CRESSMAN   Dennis Donecker   MITCH EASTER   Sandy Evans Jolonen   Tammie Faircloth   Terri Faircloth
JASON FERGUSON   W. David Foster   BECKY & CHRIS GIBSON   Daniel Gill   COREY GLOVER   STEVE GORMAN   Alan Grey   STEVEN HALEY
RICKY HATTAWAY   CHRISTOPHER HOOKER   Patrick Hughes   SHELTON HULL   Rena Hyde Witkowski   SUEN JOHNSON
John Jones   Katie Jones   Eileen Kerr Haley   BRIAN KEELE   Kevn Kinney   DAWN KILBERG   Nikki Kragiel   JEN KROST AdOLPH
VICTOR KRUMMENACHER   Jim Leatherman   SCOTT LEUTHOLD   KIM LOACH FLOYD   JUDY MARENISS   John Marshall   BRYAN MASSEY
Mikey Mayhem   JAMES MCCAFFREY   Courtenay McLeland   Jo Meszaros   Max Michaels   BETH MIHALY   Laura Minor
CHRIS MONDIA   Julie Morris   MARK MULCAHY   RAY NEAL   Hope Nicholls   MOJO NIXON   GREG O'REAR   DANNA PENTES   Steve Pomberg
MISSY PONDER   Joe Popp   JAMES QUINE   Susannah Ramsey   Denise Reagan   Kristin Terrell Reeder   TERESA RENFROE
Ben Reynolds   DAN RICHMOND   Tony Rojas   DARREN RONAN   MELANIE RYDER   Tonya Santa Cruz Donati   EDDIE SANCHEZ
MORGAN SAPP   DENNY SCOTT   Jonathan Segal   STEPHANIE SEYMOUR   Tracy Shedd   Patrick Sheehan   Kimberley Shepard
CHRIS STESEN   Errol Stewart   JIM SOMMER   Mike Spain   SCOTT STARRATT   CATINA JANE STOVER GRAY   Christina Stuller   JOE
JACK TALCUM   JENNY THOMAS MEDURE   ERIN & CHRIS TOMASKI   Bruce J. Tomecko   JAY TOTTY   Joel Totty   STEPHANIE TOTTY
Meredith Tousey Matthews   Michael Triplett   James Tritten   RYAN & ANGELA TURK   William Tutton   MICHAEL VIRZERA
Rodney Walker   DOUG WALTONBAUGH   DAWNIE WALTON   Adam Watson   MIKE WATT   JOHN WEBB   NATASHA WEIMANN
Armistead Wellford   MARIANNA WHANG   Neil Wheeler   ROBIN WHETSTONE   Siobhan White   Melody White-Crinon
Michael Whittier   JIM WILBUR   Emily Wilder   ANDREW PAUL WILLIAMS   Jacquie Wojcik   PALMER WOOD   SHANNON WRIGHT

SPECIAL THANKS TO

SHAWN BARTON VACH, Erin Carson, OSHA GILLESPIE, Kristen Morgan, Jeffrey Totty

We would also like to thank everyone who made a contribution to *Occupancy 250*.
Whether it was a photo, interview, flier, ticket stub or quote, we appreciate
everything you shared that helped make this a thorough and heartfelt
collection worthy of our beloved Einstein A Go-Go.

Lee Ranaldo from Sonic Youth
with Jim Leatherman, Sun Ray
Cinema in Jax, 2022

"In 1986 I went to Gainesville to see Sonic Youth and struck up a conversation with Lee Ranaldo about photography because he liked my camera. He said, 'We're playing in Jacksonville tomorrow. I don't know how far that is away from here or wherever you're from, but we'll put you on the guest list.' So a friend and I drove up to Einstein's and we got there at 6. We got to hang out and watch them do the soundcheck. I worked up the courage to ask if they would be willing to pose for some pictures, and they're like 'Yeah, sure. That'd be awesome.'"

— JIM LEATHERMAN

Check out page 40

PHOTO CONTRIBUTERS

Robert Armstrong: Nirvana *(152)*; Tad *(159)*

Zachary Boyle: Velocity Girl, Fuzzy *(165)*

Zak Champagne: Buffalo Tom, St. Johnny *(162)*

Jennifer Curry Compton: The Connells *(90)*; Jonathyne Briggs *(188)*; Ricky Hattaway *(189)*; Matt Hopkins *(190)*; Chris Stesen *(191)*; Terri and Chris Stesen *(202)*; Freak Scene *(233-236)*

Allison Durham: Love Tractor *(32-35)*; Living Colour *(42, 148-151)*; Beat Rodeo *(48)*; Swans *(49)*; Camper Van Beethoven *(50-53)*; The Dead Milkmen *(57-59)*; Miracle Legion *(60-61)*; Bodeans *(69)*; Beggar Weeds *(72-74)*; Bell Book and Candle *(76)*; Pie Wackit *(77)*; Aleka's Attic *(84-85)*; Let's Active *(86-87)*; Fetchin Bones *(92-97)*; The dB's *(98)*; The Veldt *(101)*; Mary My Hope *(103)*; Kilkenny Cats *(104-105)*; Hetch Hetchy *(106-107)*; Dreams So Real *(108)*; Indigo Girls *(112)*; Pylon *(113-115)*; Faith No More *(116-117)*; Fishbone *(118-119)*; Brian Brain *(124-125)*; Now Explosion *(131)*; They Might Be Giants *(132)*; Pili Pili *(133)*; Robyn Hitchcock *(136-139)*; Jane's Addiction *(140-141)*; Hugo Largo *(142-143)*; Book of Love *(144)*; Royal Crescent Mob *(146)*; It's Snakes *(244)*; Mike Watt *(244)*; Corey Glover *(245)*; Armistead Wellford *(246)*; Pylon Reenactment Society *(246)*

Tammie Faircloth: Einstein's stage *(242-243)*

Jason Ferguson: Das Damen *(158)*

Charles Furment: rickoLus *(245)*

Steven Haley: Common Thread *(244)*

Brian Keele: Gothic and Lee'A Fawl *(83)*

Jim Leatherman: Horsechild Breakfast *(31)*; Sonic Youth *(40-41, 64-65)*; 10,000 Maniacs *(44-45)*; The Reivers *(56)*; The Replacements *(54)*; Alex Chilton *(55)*; fIREHOSE *(64-67)*; Crowsdell *(75)*; The Connells *(88-89)*; Hope Nicholls *(92)*; Guadalcanal Diary *(109)*; Chompfish *(110)*; Drivin N Cryin *(111)*; Henry Rollins *(122)*; Soul Asylum *(154-155)*; John and Mary *(160-161)*; The Cranberries *(166-169)*; Tommy Stinson *(246)*

Riccardo Livorni, 123rf: Records *(36-37)*

Kristen Morgan: Tammie making fliers *(25)*; Common Thread *(79)*; Superchunk *(99)*; Bruce Tomecko *(190)*; 2011 reunion *(249-250)*

Joe Popp: One Minute Father *(266)*

James Quine: Faircloth family *(10)*; dance floor *(12-13)*; Sonic Youth *(62-63)*; B.A.L.L. *(70-71)*; club kids *(172-173)*; Sonic Youth with Willie Idle *(212)*; Ralph Williams *(264-265)*

Kristin Terrill Reeder: hanging light, candy machines, record bin *(232)*

Teresa Renfroe: Modern English *(127)*

Darren Ronan: Cotton Box *(82)*; EAGG exterior *(263)*

Scott Starratt: Mike Watt *(68)*

James Tritten: Les Claypool *(159)*

John Webb: The Long Drive Home *(240-241)*

Siobhan White: 2006 reunion *(248)*

Jacquie Wojcik: The Flaming Lips *(245)*

Photographs copyright by the original photographers

DID YOU KNOW?

"John Lombardo got a little tipsy after a 10,000 Maniacs show and decided to steal the arm of the mannequin we named 'Harold.' Why? I don't think he even knows. Apparently Harold's arm was packed into their gear and traveled with the band on their world tour. When the band showed up the next time, John sheepishly handed it back to me and apologized emphatically. We had John sign the arm and then returned it to Harold's bust. I have no idea where it is to this day."

— TAMMIE FAIRCLOTH

The REPLACEMENTS started their national tour, the first in four years, at the club with the reputation of being the best in Florida, EINSTEIN A GO GO.

10,000 Maniacs included live recordings of "Gun Shy" and "Like The Weather" from their Einstein's show on Dec. 13, 1987, on the B-side of the U.K. 12-inch and CD-single releases of "What's the Matter Here?"

268

MEET THE AUTHORS

Allison Durham

Since her Einstein's days, Allison has traveled the country as a circus clown, got a degree in photojournalism from UF, and worked as a reporter. She lives in a hundred-year-old house with an orange cat in Georgia. She enjoys writing, traveling and working on cosplay costumes.

FAVORITE SHOWS *Living Colour, Fetchin Bones, Pylon, Now Explosion*

CLUB STYLE *I used to dress up then I realized to dance is to sweat and I switched to jeans and T-shirts*

Jon Glass

Having segued professionally from Florida's newspaper industry to academia, Jon teaches digital journalism at Syracuse University's S.I. Newhouse School of Public Communications. Still very much an avid music fan, Jon catches as many concerts as he can especially for any up-and-coming acts that roll through upstate New York. He's all ears for any musical recommendations you have.

FAVORITE SHOWS *Camper Van Beethoven, Fetchin Bones, Pylon, Sonic Youth, They Might Be Giants*

CLUB STYLE *Concert tee (likely R.E.M. Pageantry tour) or Gap clearance rack shirt, baggie jeans and some scuffed brown leather kicks*

Dee Edenfield Marling

After Einstein's, Dee (a.k.a. in EAGG scene as *D2* or *D-Square*) has rocked a career in the business world and enjoys keeping the club's spirit alive through co-organizing the reunions, EAGG Facebook group and scheming fresh ways to unite the Einstein's crew. Dee calls Jacksonville home along with her husband, kids and a couple of cool cats.

FAVORITE SHOWS *Sonic Youth, Fetchin Bones, fIREHOSE, Guadalcanal Diary, Camper Van Beethoven*

CLUB STYLE *Edge City black skirt, concert T-shirt (New Order or Joy Division, of course), oversized vintage men's button-up, black karate shoes or black boots, antique earrings and black eyeliner*

Jennifer Curry Compton

Jennifer has enjoyed a career as a graphic designer working primarily on magazines and books. She lives in Jacksonville with her cats in a historic home filled with brightly-colored vintage décor. Her record album, cassette tape and CD collections are still intact.

FAVORITE SHOWS *The Connells, Fetchin Bones, Jane Siberry, Mojo Nixon, The Cranberries*

CLUB STYLE *Edge City pajama pants, baby doll shoes, black azure hair dye, ankh earrings, vintage dresses*

INDEX

EINSTEIN
a CO-CO
327 N 1° ST.

1985-1997